Taunton's
BUILD LIKE A PRO®
Expert Advice from Start to Finish

REMODELING A
BATHROOM

Expert Advice from Start to Finish

REMODELING A
BATHROOM

LEON A. FRECHETTE

The Taunton Press

The Taunton Press
Inspiration for hands-on living®

The Taunton Press, Inc., 63 South Main Street, P.O. Box 5506, Newtown, CT 06470-5506
e-mail: tp@taunton.com

EDITOR: Erica Sanders-Foege
COVER DESIGN: Lori Wendin
INTERIOR DESIGN: Lori Wendin
LAYOUT: Jeff Potter/Potter Publishing Studio
ILLUSTRATOR: Mario Ferro

Taunton's Build Like a Pro® is a trademark of The Taunton Press, Inc.,
registered in the U.S. Patent and Trademark Office.

Library of Congress Cataloging-in-Publication Data

Frechette, Leon A., 1954–
  Remodeling a bathroom / Leon A. Frechette.
     p. cm. -- (Taunton's build like a pro)
Includes index.
  ISBN 1-56158-621-8
  1. Bathrooms--Remodeling. I. Title. II. Series.
TH4816.3.B37F76 2004
643'.52--dc22
                          2003025282

Printed in the United States of America
10 9 8 7 6 5 4 3

To my wife Kimberly, whose design expertise and infinite patience finally paid off.

Acknowledgments

A book of this size and nature doesn't happen overnight. It takes a lot of planning and hard work. It can also take, as it did in our case, some hardship—we have only one bathroom. My wife Kimberly, an interior designer, has been through a lot of projects with me, and this one almost pushed her very understanding nature and high tolerance to the limit. In the end, she pulled together our entire 1930s theme and created a wonderfully nostalgic environment. At Christmas (2002) she got her bathroom—and she loves it!

Kimberly and I are grateful to Pat Herrin and our son Kevan McClarty, who opened their homes—and showers—to us.

I want to thank Karen Craig for her dedicated work in organizing, editing, and proofreading our sixth book together. I also thank Calvin Lea from L.P.S. Photo-Graphics in Spokane, Washington. This project, our first collaboration, came to life through his lens. Every writer should be lucky enough to have an editor and photographer willing to share both expertise and friendship. It makes the whole process enjoyable.

I would like to give special thanks to the following people: Tom Craig, certified plans examiner of Spokane, Washington, for the time he spent, after hours, reading text and reviewing diagrams to make sure they met code requirements; to the project inspector, Jim Cooley, a certified building and plumbing inspector of Spokane, for reviewing plumbing diagrams and for his expertise with the plumbing rough-in; and Terry Danzer, certified electrical and mechanical inspector of Spokane, for taking the time to review the diagrams concerning electrical codes.

I especially want to thank the following manufacturers involved in this project: Terry J. Gibbons with The Swan® Corporation; Ken Brock with PricePfister®; Debbie Richter and Todd Weber with Kohler® Co.; Gary Good with Hy-Lite Products, Inc.; Rob Voigt with Deflect-o® Corporation; Mark Fries with SunTouch®; Charles Scott with Jacuzzi® Whirlpool Bath; Dennis Bright with Johns Manville; Paul Fitzmaurice representing Dap Inc.; Katie Caratelli representing Waterpik® Technologies; Alissa Calder and Peter Hayward of RIDGID® Tool Company; Susan White with Zinsser®; Sil Argentin with Bosch Tools; Todd Langston of Porter-Cable; and Andy Fox representing Stanley®/Goldblatt®.

Finally, I'd like to thank those suppliers close to home: Carleen Primm with Pro Source Wholesale Floor Coverings in Spokane, for her help in selecting the right tiles; and Joey Marcella with Mario & Son, Inc. in Spokane, for fabricating the wonderful iguana granite countertop—a job well done!

Contents

Introduction

GROWING UP I was privileged to learn a few things from my grandfather, who had been a carpenter in the service, and from my mom, who was a contractor wannabe. I just never knew what our house would look like when I got home from school—that was my early introduction to remodeling. Little has changed today. My wife Kimberly is an interior designer, so I never know when I leave for a trip if we'll still have the same furniture when I return. Nevertheless, we make a good team.

When I got my contractor's license in 1976, at the age of 22, I had to pretend to be an expert in my field in order to get the experience that eventually made me one. That was hard to do at first; I missed out on a lot of jobs because I looked too young to be a remodeling contractor. I learned along the way that I loved to remodel and build new bathrooms. I knew I could make a difference in a 5-ft. by 9-ft. space, the typical size for an average bathroom.

I have written before about bathroom remodeling, but this book project was especially appealing because it presented the opportunity to gut a bathroom and completely renovate it. (We've lived in our house 18 years and have never done any major remodeling.) I enjoyed working with my wife to create a new bathroom with a 1930s nostalgic feel. It was a complicated project that took months of planning: finding the right products and fixtures; contracting for custom work; and purchasing items and supplies so they'd be on hand when needed. The planning was worth the time invested, as you can see by the photographs on the cover and throughout the book.

The hands-on experience I bring to *Build Like a Pro: Remodel Your Bathroom* is documented by text, illustrations, and photos. I wrote the book specifically to help you, the homeowner, understand the proper way to start a project and learn the steps required to finish the work. Because the book paints a realistic picture of what it takes to remodel a bathroom, you'll be able to make intelligent decisions about the scope of your project. Use the book as tool to help you understand or visualize the remodeling process. You will learn that itemizing a job can help you perform the work in the proper sequence for a smooth and efficient project.

Your work schedule needs to comply with the building, electrical, and plumbing codes established and enforced by your local building department. Be aware that electrical and plumbing permits, as well as inspections, sometimes fall under state rather than city or county jurisdiction. Be sure to check requirements in your municipality.

The information contained in this book is intended to be a resource for you. It's not the final word. The best advice I can give is to take the time to read the entire book to get a feel for what it will take to remodel your bathroom completely. Good luck with your project, no matter how large or small!

How to Use This Book

F YOU'RE READING THIS, you're a doer, not afraid to take on a challenging project. We designed this book and this series to help you get that project done smoothly and cost effectively.

Many doers jump in and do, reading the directions only if something goes wrong. It's much smarter (and cheaper) to start with knowing what to do and planning the process step by step. This book is here to help you. Read it. Familiarize yourself with the process you're about to undertake. You'll be glad you did.

Planning Is the Key to Success

This book contains information on designing your project, choosing the best options for the results you want to achieve, and planning the timing and execution. We know you're anxious to get started on your project. Take the time now to read and think about what you're setting out to do. You'll refine your ideas and choose the best materials.

There's advice here on where to look for inspiration and how to make plans. Don't be afraid to make an attempt at drawing your own plans. There's no better way to get exactly what you want than by designing it yourself. If you think you need the assistance of an architect or engineer, you'll find advice in this book on why and how to work with these professionals.

After you've decided what you're going to undertake, make lists of materials, and budget both your money and your time. There's nothing more annoying than a project that goes on forever.

Finding the Information You Need

We've designed this book to make it easy to find what you need to know. The main part of the book details the essential parts of each process. If it's fairly straightforward, it's simply described. If there are key steps, these are addressed one by one and usually accompanied by drawings or photos to help you see what you will be doing. We've also added some other elements to help you understand the process better, find quicker or smarter ways to accomplish the task, or do it differently to suit your project.

Alternatives and a closer look

The sidebars and features included with the main text are there to explain aspects in more depth and to clarify why you're doing something. In some cases, they are used to describe a completely different way of handling the same situation. We explain the advantages of this alternative method or option so that you can decide if you want to use it. Sidebars are usually accompanied by photos or drawings to help you see what the author is describing. They're meant to help, but they're not essential to understanding or doing the work.

Heads up!

We urge you to read the "Safety First" and "According to Code" sidebars we've included. "Safety First" gives you a warning about hazards that can harm or even kill you. Always work safely. Use appropriate safety aids and know what you're doing before you start work. Don't take unnecessary chances, and if a procedure makes you uncomfortable, try to find another way to do it. "According to Code" can save you from trouble with your building inspector, building an unsafe structure, or having to rip your project apart and build it again to suit the local codes.

There's a pro at your elbow

The author of this book, and every author in this series, has had years of experience doing this kind of project. We've put the benefits of their knowledge in shaded columns that always appear in the left margin. "Pro Tips" are ideas or insights that will save you time or money. "In Detail" is a short explanation of an aspect that may be of interest to you. While not essential to getting the job done, these features are meant to explain some "whys."

Every project has its surprises. Since the author has encountered many of them already, he can give you a little preview of what they may be and how to address them. And experience has also taught the author some tricks he's willing to share. Some of these are tips about tools or accessories you can make yourself, or about a material or tool you may not have thought to use.

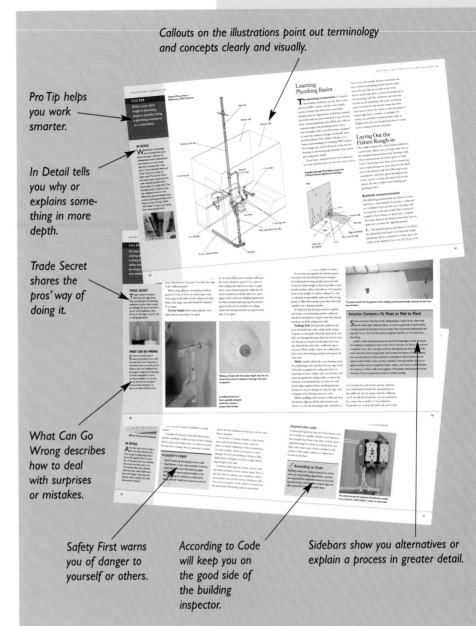

Callouts on the illustrations point out terminology and concepts clearly and visually.

Pro Tip helps you work smarter.

In Detail tells you why or explains something in more depth.

Trade Secret shares the pros' way of doing it.

What Can Go Wrong describes how to deal with surprises or mistakes.

Safety First warns you of danger to yourself or others.

According to Code will keep you on the good side of the building inspector.

Sidebars show you alternatives or explain a process in greater detail.

Building Like a Pro

To make a living, a pro needs to work smart, quickly, and cost-effectively. That's the strategy presented in this book. We've provided options to help you make the best choices in design, materials, and methods. That way you can adjust your project to suit your skill level and budget. Good choices and good planning are the keys to success. And remember that the knowledge and skill you acquire on this project will make the next one easier.

Repair or

CHAPTER ONE
Remodel?

Most of my potential customers call and say, "I'd like to have a new tub." What they don't realize is that replacing a tub is almost as expensive as redoing the whole bathroom because it requires opening three walls and possibly moving fixtures and cabinetry. Once they understand that, they face a choice: find an alternative to replacing the tub or remodel the whole bathroom.

You may be facing similar decisions. Maybe you'd like to make a few repairs, such as replacing broken tiles, leaking faucets, and tilting toilets. The room may need a facelift—new tile, fresh paint, and a new countertop. Perhaps a full remodel is in order. You might want to add space or rearrange fixtures. Regardless of the project's scale, taking the bath out of use will be a major household disruption—it is, after all, one of the busiest rooms in the house.

The keys to a successful remodeling project are knowing your capabilities and planning. Before you tear into your walls, begin by carefully evaluating your current bathroom.

PRO TIP

If you think your toilet's leaking at the base, add food coloring to the tank and flush. If there is a leak, you'll see tinted water seeping on the floor.

TRADE SECRET

To detect other sources of leakage, go to the basement or crawlspace and look for water damage on the ceiling or underside of the subfloor near water lines and drainpipes. If the ceiling is wet, cut a small inspection hole using a hand wallboard keyhole saw. Water could be trapped in this area and your hole may unplug the dam, so beware. Inspect the area using a bright flashlight. Also look for water creeping down drainpipes, especially after someone has used the plumbing.

WHAT CAN GO WRONG

The water damage on the outside of this tub could have been caused by an improperly closed shower curtain, water leaking under a shower door track, or leakage from a plumbing pipe. This type of damage can occur at both ends of a tub/shower.

This sink uses an S-trap for a drain, which doesn't meet plumbing codes. The S-trap design allows siphoning to start during draining which eventually will drain the trap and allow sewer gases to enter the home. (Photo © Leon A. Frechette)

Evaluating the Project

Until you get into demolition, it's difficult to get a handle on exactly how much work will be required to design and construct your dream bathroom. Begin with an inspection: evaluate your plumbing, and look for water damage and outdated or worn-out fixtures. Then consider the cabinets, lighting, and ventilation. Perhaps you need to rearrange or enlarge the bath to accommodate users with special needs. You will also want to consider the amount of time you have to devote to the project. Finally, work out a budget. If you take the project one step at a time, you'll be able to lay out a realistic plan.

Water damage

Water damage, the biggest factor in determining the size of the project, will take some detective work to accurately assess. Sometimes water damage is obvious—a "spongy" floor, blistering paint, loose tiles, or a stained wall surface. Start by examining the floor around the base of the toilet. It may feel spongy and give way underfoot, or you may see signs of water coming up

With a leak like this, it's just a matter of time before the ceiling falls down due to the weight of the water absorbed by the wallboard.

between the floor tiles. Discoloration of the flooring could indicate a leak or simply be due to a colored contour rug.

It could also be caused by the toilet's wax ring being worn out, broken, or incorrectly set, or by a cracked or broken flange. Other possibilities could include cracks in the toilet base or toilet drain

The cause of this leak was the wax ring, damaged during a previous installation.

This faucet has been leaking into the claw-foot tub for some time, judging by the stain on the bottom of the tub underneath it. (Photo © Leon A. Frechette)

horn that the wax ring fits over. Don't overlook the possibility that your fixture has a hairline crack or that it came defective from the factory.

Look for loose tiles, water-marked wood or vinyl, or flooring that's curled up at the edge where the floor meets the front of the tub/shower area. Water may be leaking under the shower curtain or, if you have one, at the door track where it meets the walls. The bead of caulk between the floor and tub/shower area may be loose, allowing water to seep through.

The main plumbing wall—where the plumbing valve for the faucets, shower head, or tub spout is located—is another area to check. Look for loose tiles about two feet above the

tub/shower area, or along the outside of the tub down to the floor. Other signs include blistering paint, mildew, and loose wallboard. There may be a leak in the plumbing fittings and/or valve.

Windows in the shower area almost always cause water damage. A wooden window can absorb (or wick) water as you shower. If this has happened in your bathroom, you'll see water stains in the corners and two or three inches up the frame. Loose tiles below the window, and staining or a spongy feel to the interior and exterior walls, indicate that water is leaking down through the window ledge or sill.

Upgrading fixtures

When it comes to eye appeal, a fresh remodel always trumps a tired bath with worn-out fixtures. The key is to keep it simple. As you plan your project, don't lose sight of resale value. At some point you may sell your home, and an upgraded bathroom might add to the selling price. You can replace worn out or dated fixtures with new reproductions to maintain the integrity of the home's style. Water stains, chipped countertops, missing porcelain, and rust on tubs and sinks are

✚ SAFETY FIRST

If you have to cut an inspection hole in the ceiling to check for water damage, be sure to wear safety goggles to protect your eyes from falling debris.

Our bathroom has had a wooden window in the shower area since 1932. Eventually, water leaked down the wallboard, causing damage to studs and exterior siding.

TRADE SECRET

A spongy feel to a wall containing the soap holder indicates that water might have leaked behind it, especially if it's a metal fixture in a tile wall. Inside, check for loose tiles between the soap holder and the top of the tub/shower pan. Remove the metal fixture and replace it with a ceramic one for a tighter seal.

(Photo © Leon A. Frechette)

IN DETAIL

A fan that runs only as long as you're in the shower lacks time to get its siphoning action up to full capacity. Turn on your fan 15 minutes prior to a shower and crack the door. Let it run 15 minutes after your shower with the door open. Bathroom fans with higher cubic feet per minute (cfm) ratings vent odor and moisture better.

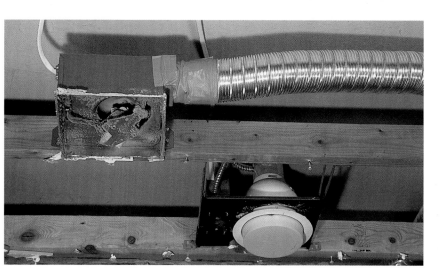

The upwardly bent duct in this old bathroom fan trapped moisture.

indications that it's time to refurbish or make repairs.

Consider the faucets in the tub/shower area and the washbasin. If they are out of style, leaking, hard to use, or just plain worn out, then it's probably time for a change. You can purchase a quality

+ SAFETY FIRST

Even if replacing lead piping is not a code requirement in your area, consider it anyway, especially if you have disturbed any pipes (which could cause expensive leaks in the future). It may be costly but is well worth doing, both for health and economic reasons.

faucet for the washbasin for the price of two visits from a plumber.

If you have a wooden window in the shower area—and decide that you really need one there—consider replacing it with an aluminum or vinyl window, which is less prone to water damage. If you're just looking to bring in light, think about a skylight, or acrylic or glass blocks placed high in the wall.

Consider replacing your vanity cabinet with one that's prebuilt or even custom made. Now is also the time to evaluate your medicine cabinet (if you have one) and the mirror. Medicine cabinets can be mounted on the wall or recessed into the stud cavity. Recessing requires some planning, but it alone can change the overall look of your bathroom.

When people enter a room, they normally form their first impression by looking at the floor, so carefully evaluate yours. Even if you feel there's nothing wrong with it, it's most likely outdated.

I've given you a lot to consider. If you're feeling overwhelmed, consult a design professional.

Meeting codes

Whatever's in your bathroom that doesn't meet current building, electrical, mechanical, and plumbing codes will now need to be updated. Anything altered, added, or rebuilt has to meet local building requirements—meaning you must have permits for this project. For example, if your existing bathroom doesn't have an exhaust fan, you'll be required to install one when you remodel. You may have to install a Ground Fault Circuit Interrupter (GFCI) outlet. There's a lot to think about, so start a checklist to keep you on track.

Beyond the code

It always feels good to step out of the shower into the warmth, so consider whether your bathroom has enough heat. Now is the time to think about supplementing the system you already have, perhaps with a heat lamp, a heater installed in the toekick of the vanity cabinet, or radiant heat located in the floor.

✔ According to Code

Building codes vary widely so be sure to check with your local building department—permits are required. The inspections done by the building department will keep your project legal and safe, which also helps with resale value.

Frequently the light in a bathroom is insufficient, or perhaps the lighting fixtures are improperly located. Think about moving fixtures or perhaps adding specialized fixtures such as track lighting, recessed lighting, and bar lights. An improperly located electrical outlet can make an entire bathroom inconvenient and uncomfortable. Consider moving existing outlets, adding more outlets, and converting ungrounded outlets to grounded ones.

If you don't already have a water softener, you may want to consider installing this device to protect new fixtures, including your hot-water tank, from the mineral deposits created by hard water. Hard water may damage plumbing. It also wastes soap, detergents, and shampoos. Future savings in consumer products and repairs could make a water softener a smart investment. To determine the hardness of your water, contact your local water-softening service about getting the water tested. Alternatively, search for "hard water" on the Internet and purchase an in-home test kit.

The electrical permit requires all bathroom outlets to be wired to a GFCI (left) in order to meet code.

PRO TIP

Photocopy "before" and "after" floor plans and cut out the shapes of the various fixtures and cabinets. Create a floor plan by arranging and rearranging them.

TRADE SECRET

Put otherwise unusable space to work by installing a heater (or a vent from your heating system) in the toekick of your vanity cabinet. Be sure to check code requirements with your building department to ensure a safe installation. Or look into an electric floor-warming system, which is discussed in Chapter Four.

IN DETAIL

As you work through your project, write down questions for your local building officials. Don't try to get all your answers over the phone. Instead, make an appointment to speak with someone in person, and leave plenty of time to discuss your questions. Take your drawings, diagrams, and pictures with you—they will help you get the answers you need. Be sure to take written notes—don't count on remembering all the details.

With new plumbing upstairs and the need to replace the cast iron soil pipe, this area of the concrete floor had to be removed to permit full access to waste pipes below the concrete. This is no easy task and requires some not-so-average tools—an electric jackhammer, for example, or a rotary hammer.

Creating a Floor Plan

This evaluation process may seem drawn out, but it's important to dissect the project so you can create a realistic blueprint. From that floor plan, you'll be able to make a detailed materials list, which will allow you to calculate the costs. The floor plan will also shed light on how much energy it will take to complete this project. However, before you create a floor plan, let me point out other important concerns you need to address.

The test case

A bathroom remodeling—my wife Kimberly's and mine—was commissioned especially for this book, and most of the photos in it were taken during this project. Our home has one bathroom—on the main floor—located above an unfinished area in the basement where our laundry facilities are housed.

Remodeling according to my floor plan required relocating plumbing, replacing an electric hot-water tank, and breaking up the concrete floor in the basement to install a new floor drain

Main Floor Bathroom, Before and After
Reconfiguring the space created a more user-friendly environment.

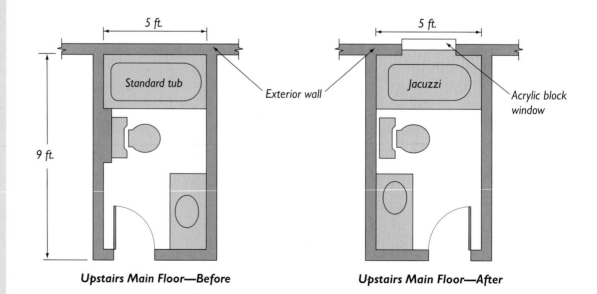

Upstairs Main Floor—Before

Upstairs Main Floor—After

MAKING SPACE FOR A LARGER BATHROOM

To reach the pipes, the concrete was broken up with a jackhammer and the soil removed using this drain spade.

If you're thinking of enlarging your bathroom, consider the following:

- It is easier to access plumbing and electrical work for a main-floor bathroom since there is usually a basement or crawlspace located beneath it.

- Second-floor bathrooms are more expensive to install because you'll need a longer hookup to the soil pipe (waste), also called the main stack, and you might also need to lower a ceiling to conceal both waste and supply (water) lines. A basement bathroom could be just as expensive, especially if rough-in plumbing needs to be installed.

- Consider the rooms surrounding the bathroom you want to enlarge. A bigger bathroom will mean a smaller adjacent room or the loss of a closet or bedroom. Space taken from a nearby room to enlarge the bathroom may detract from the resale value of the home.

- It may make more sense to add a second bathroom elsewhere in the home, rather than remodel your existing bathroom. From a cost standpoint, it's best to put bathrooms back-to-back or one above the other.

- If you plan to install a new bathroom, first locate the main stack. The farther away from the main stack you locate a bathroom, the harder it is to aesthetically conceal the soil pipe's proper 1/4-in. to 1-ft. downward drainage slope without jeopardizing the code-required ceiling height. Therefore, the overall installation will be more expensive.

Back-to-Back Baths
This simple three-piece bathroom off a master bedroom illustrates back-to-back plumbing and features convenient location of laundry facilities.

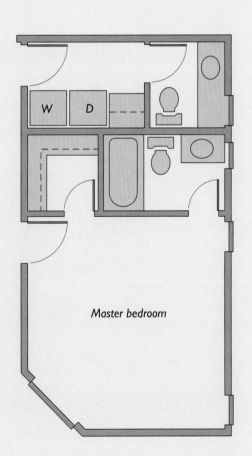

PRO TIP

A scale layout for a typical 5-ft. × 9-ft. bathroom fits nicely on one sheet of graph paper with 1/2-in. by 1/2-in. grids (one grid equals 6 in.).

IN DETAIL

If you now find showering in a bathtub to be inconvenient, uncomfortable, or unsafe, replace the tub with a shower pan that fits the existing opening. No framing will be required, but you will need to remove the surfaces on the three surrounding walls and install a new shower enclosure and door. Shower pans with left- or right-hand drains to fit existing drain hookups eliminate the need for replumbing the drain. Take advantage of having the plumbing wall open to replace the tub valve with a shower valve or to plug off the tub spigot. The Swan product shown here allows easy walk-in or wheelchair access.

(Photo: The Swan Corporation)

for the hot-water tank. With the concrete open, we decided to install vent pipes for a future second bath. It's simply more cost-effective. Even if you don't have resources to put in a second bathroom now, I recommend that you complete as much of its rough-in plumbing as you can; that way you won't end up breaking out the concrete slab more than once.

As you plan your bathroom project, consider the following:

- If you have penciled in a new bathtub, shower, whirlpool-type tub, or hot tub, know the dimensions of the unit you have chosen.
- You will need to know the dimensions of your shower pan, especially if you plan to custom make a unit. The code requires a shower pan that is a minimum of 1,024 sq. in. (32 in. by 32 in.) and able to contain a 30-in. circle within the pan. If you are replacing an existing shower pan that is smaller than this, in most cases (depending on the inspector), you'll be able to use one that is the same size as the original.
- Be sure to allow room for the shower door to swing out and the main door to swing in. You may need to relocate the bathroom door.
- Know the dimensions of the bathroom cabinet you plan to install.
- It is easier and more economical to keep all the plumbing fixtures on the same wall.

+ SAFETY FIRST

When installing a wall-hung washbasin for a wheelchair user, insulate both water-supply lines and the drainpipe to protect the user's legs from hot temperatures and rough, hard surfaces.

- If there is a room above the new bathroom, it may be possible to conceal the plumbing in its closet or in one of its walls.

Sometimes plumbing is difficult to figure out. Don't hesitate to hire a plumber as a consultant, or even to perform some of the work, if that's what your project warrants.

Now let's take everything up to this point and incorporate it into a floor plan.

Design and layout

Before drawing your floor plan, consider using planning (graph) paper with 1/4-in. by 1/4-in. grid-lines and an architect's triangular scale. You can also use a 12-in. standard ruler. Another timesaving tool is a template designed with house-plan symbols, including door swings, cabinets, bathroom fixtures, and many others. These templates,

Working with a template can simplify the drawing of plumbing fixtures, door openings, and cabinets.

scaled from ⅛ in. to ½ in., are inexpensive and can be purchased at most art supply stores. If you have the time, the resources, and a computer, you may find specialized home-design software helpful.

Once you have your basic information outlined, you're ready to begin. You will want to make two drawings: one of your bathroom exactly as it now exists with every measurement marked down, and one of your new design. As you draw your floor plans, take another look at the plans I've included for reference. With all the suggestions I provide throughout this book, you have lots to consider in your new design.

Drape openings with plastic to contain the dust created by plaster and lath demolition. Work slowly and wear a mask.

Special Designs for Special Needs

Barrier-free design accommodates people with disabilities or special needs but poses a challenge for those remodeling—mostly because special-needs people require more space.

Start with a roll-in shower that fits within the dimensions of a standard tub. Since it doesn't have a lip, there's more floor space for maneuvering a wheelchair or walker. This design can provide accessibility in an area where space is limited. A roll-in shower also provides sufficient room for a "T-turn."

For a more special-needs-friendly bathroom, install lever-type door and loop or lever-type faucet handles, low mirrors, non-skid floors, accessible toilets, and grab bars. The National Easter Seal Society, Eastern Paralyzed Veterans Association, and the Department of Justice—regarding the Americans with Disabilities Act (ADA)—have more information. Consult with your local building department to ensure that the plans you design comply with the building codes in your area.

Barrier-Free Bathrooms
These two barrier-free bathroom designs permit a "diagonal approach" to the toilet for a wheelchair user.

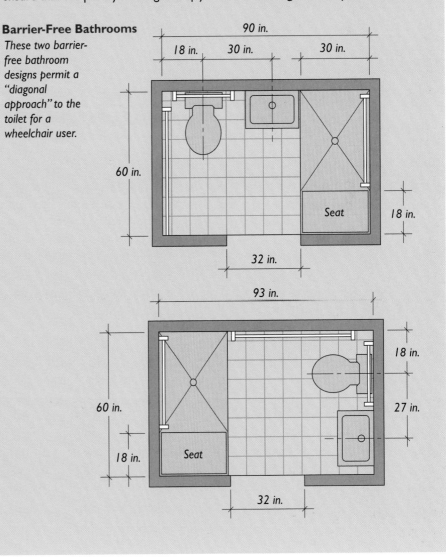

IN DETAIL

These basic fixture measurements are helpful in planning your bathroom:

- A standard bathtub is 60 in. long and 30 in. wide.

- A toilet requires a minimum of 24 in. of space in front of the bowl, but 30 in. is preferable.

- A vanity cabinet must be a minimum of 24 in. wide to accommodate a washbasin.

- A door should be a minimum of 30 in. wide.

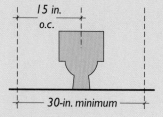

15 in.
o.c.

30-in. minimum

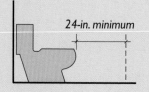

24-in. minimum

Gauging the Scope of Work

Drawing the floor plan is the easiest part of the project. Assessing your abilities, working out a budget, and selecting materials present much bigger challenges. Take your time evaluating your current bathroom. It's important now to try to draw as clear a picture as possible about the scope of your project.

There are many things still to consider. Sometimes changing one item will require you to remove three others. For example, replacing floor covering means you've got to pull out the toilet and replace the wax ring and possibly the toilet flange. Most likely you'll need to remove the old underlayment and install a new one. All rubber or wooden base molding will have to be pried away before the floor and underlayment can be removed.

Replacing the tub may seem like an attractive option, but it often requires opening up three walls to remove the existing tub. If the room is small, the toilet, washbasin, and cabinet may also need to be removed. You may also need to take off the base moldings, floor covering, and underlayment.

If you have a room with a finished ceiling under the bath, you may have to open up that ceiling to reach plumbing or wiring or to look for leaks.

Skills, experience, and your time

Only you know how much of the remodeling work you are capable of doing, so consider the following:

Three You May Need

Considering all the bathroom renovations I've worked on over the years, I've gained a real respect for subcontractors. I found that my jobs went a lot faster and easier with help from these experts:

- **Plumbers.** They know local plumbing codes, and they have the proper tools to do the job, as well as the experience to handle unexpected problems.

- **Electricians.** Since many of us are not familiar with wiring or the many complicated electrical code requirements, I recommend leaving electrical work to an expert.

- **Drywall tapers.** Taping is a slow and messy job, but these contractors are fast, they're good, and they know the real art of achieving a quality finished job.

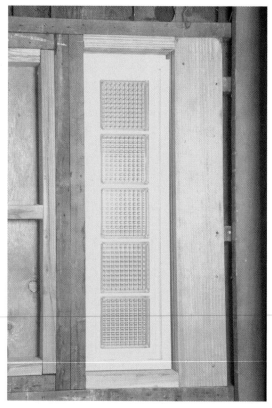

This stylish acrylic block window (Hy-Lite Products, Inc.) adds light to the shower area. Its frame is vinyl so there's no worry about paint peeling or wood absorbing water.

THE CRITICAL PATH

After you've settled on what you'd like in your new bathroom, decided how much you'll spend, consulted your local building department, and purchased your supplies and fixtures, your project should unfold like this:

Demolition and Framing (Chapter Two)

- Turn off power and water, and protect surrounding areas from dust and debris.
- Remove fixtures, walls, ceiling, and flooring.
- Remove electrical and plumbing as needed for framing.
- Frame for windows, doors, and backer boards for wallboard and fixtures.
- Install bathtub.
- Obtain framing inspection.

Rough-In Plumbing (Chapter Three)

- Lay out fixtures.
- Remove existing plumbing as needed.
- Install drain, waste and vent (DWV) system and supply lines.
- Obtain rough-in plumbing inspection.

Rough-In Electrical (Chapter Four)

- Lay out fixtures.
- Remove existing wiring as needed.
- Feed wiring and install electrical and fixture boxes.
- Test electrical system.
- Obtain rough-in electrical inspection.

Install Wallboard (Chapter Five)

- Obtain inspection for energy-code compliance.

- Correct framing as needed.
- Hang wallboard and finish walls.

Flooring, Cabinets, and Countertops (Chapter Six)

- Install underlayment, finish flooring, cabinets, and countertops.

Tub and Shower Enclosure (Chapter Seven)

- Install tub/shower enclosure.
- Case out window in tub/shower area (if applicable).

Moldings (Chapter Eight)

- Install and case out doors, case out remaining windows.
- Install base moldings.

Electrical and Plumbing Fixtures and Trims (Chapter Nine)

- Install electrical and plumbing fixtures and trim.
- Test all systems.
- Obtain final inspection of electrical, plumbing, and overall job.

Finishing Touches (Chapter Ten)

- Install door hardware, stops, and bathroom accessories.
- Caulk and do touchups.

PRO TIP

You may be able to salvage some plumbing fixtures, such as the vanity, washbasin, claw-foot tub, or vintage toilet, to sell to a used building materials dealer.

WHAT CAN GO WRONG

To cut cast iron drainpipe, use a soil pipe cutter and fit the cutting chain squarely around the pipe. Tighten the chain and use the handle to rotate it around the pipe so the cutting wheels evenly score the pipe. Again tighten the chain and rotate it around the pipe. Finally, tighten the chain until the pipe snaps. If the pipe crushes, repeat the process on either side of the break or remove the pipe completely at the nearest joint.

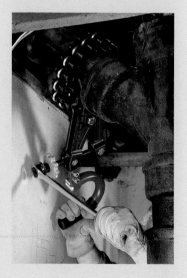

Multiple layers of flooring built up over the years forced us to tear out down to the subfloor to match up to the hallway hardwood floor and allow installation of the prehung door at the correct height.

Know-how. Remodeling your bathroom may involve dismantling it from top to bottom: disconnecting plumbing and then roughing-in according to the new plumbing plan; installing fixtures, cabinets, countertops, and wall tile; disconnecting existing electrical fixtures and roughing in new lights and outlets; and installing a ventilation fan or radiant heat. It's also likely that you'll need to install new floor covering.

+ SAFETY FIRST

When working with power tools, know at all times where your feet and fingers are. Be sure to read and follow instructions carefully. Make a habit of wearing eye and hearing protection at all times.

A tool like this right-angle drill may be more cost-effective to rent rather than buy.

Tools. Each phase of the job requires specific tools and skillful handling of them. You'll need earplugs or other hearing protection, safety goggles, a respirator, and proper work clothes—gloves, work boots, long-sleeved shirts, full-length pants, and, in some cases, a hardhat. Be sure to include this equipment in your remodeling budget. The scope of your project will dictate the tools you'll need. Pick up a few do-it-yourself magazines on bathrooms. Read about the products you might like to use so you know what to look for when pricing.

Time. Realistically assess how much time it will take to do the job. Only you know what your time is worth. Consider your availability, the inconvenience, and your comfort-level with the job.

Cost. Visit hardware and lumber stores and home centers to check out the different tools,

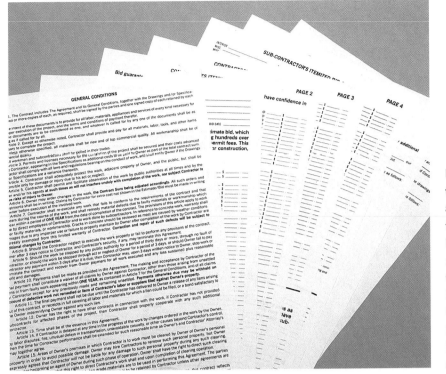

If you decide it's feasible to use a professional for all or part of the job, then ask for an itemized bid, rather than an estimate, so you see what it takes to arrive at the bottom line. The Contractor's Helping Hands Packet, shown here, is available at asktooltalk.com.

materials, products, and their costs. Keep a list of the items and their prices, and note the stores where you found them.

Don't forget to include in your calculations the costs of any permits (building, electrical, plumbing, etc.). And don't forget to add the cost of demolition, including the safe handling and disposal of hazardous materials such as asbestos and lead paint or pipes.

Materials. If you want your workmanship to last, it's important to use quality materials and treat them well. Keeping your materials indoors to

acclimatize will lessen the possibility of shrinking and warping. Use the following list as a guide for planning both your materials and your budget:

Plywood. Use sanded-face plywood marked "exterior" (stamped with APA, the trademark of The Engineered Wood Association) as an underlayment for vinyl or other resilient-finish floorings. This plywood has a special inner-ply construction with exterior glue and a solid sanded surface suitable for directly applying resilient flooring to it. It also provides dimensional stability and holds nails well.

Felt paper. Also known as "tar paper," this product provides a solid barrier between the subfloor and the underlayment. It protects against the cold and moisture of a crawl space or an unfinished basement, and it helps to eliminate squeaking floors. You can lay either 15- or 30-lb. felt between the subfloor and underlayment to match your new floor to adjoining finish flooring.

Cement board. Technically called cementitious backer board, this water-resistant product is recommended for floors, countertops, and tub/shower

---

+ SAFETY FIRST

This project will require a second pair of hands. You may think you can safely handle fixtures and construction materials, but they are too heavy and awkward for one person. As you plan, factor in extra help to maneuver materials into and around your job site. This will minimize the risk of injury to yourself and damage to your materials and property.

TRADE SECRET

Many of the building products you will use in your bathroom provide warranty protections, so be sure to read each warranty carefully and follow the manufacturer's recommended handling and installation instructions. Improper installation will void a warranty.

WHAT CAN GO WRONG

Because particleboard swells when it comes in contact with water, don't use it as an underlayment for any finish floorings. It might void the warranty on your finish-flooring material. Instead, use exterior sanded-face plywood stamped with APA, a trademark of The Engineered Wood Association. This trademark appears only on products manufactured by member mills and is the manufacturer's assurance that the products conform to the association's standards.

enclosures that may be covered by ceramic, quarry, or mosaic tiles or by thin-cut stone.

Water-resistant wallboard. This chemically-treated "green board" is designed for adhesive applications such as tub/shower enclosures and ceramic tile. It combats moisture penetration but is not waterproof; therefore, cementitious backer board is better suited for tile applications. Green board cannot be applied to an exterior wall over insulation with a vapor barrier. Another alternative backer board for tile is Dens-Shield, a gypsum

Creating a Materials List

Generic business forms can be purchased at stationery stores to help you organize your project and calculate costs, but they're usually not detailed enough to give you the total picture. If you want to know in advance where your dollars will be spent, use itemized bid sheets, as pictured on p. 19, which clearly spell out the many materials and products that might be required by your remodeling project.

product by Georgia-Pacific. Its outer surfaces contain an acrylic coating that forms a built-in vapor barrier. Embedded underneath the acrylic coating are glass mats on front and back that provide strength as well as moisture-, mold-, and mildew-resistance.

Gypsum wallboard. Standard gypsum wallboard, installed over 2×4 and 2×6 framing members or over existing walls and ceilings, is not recommended for use in areas where there is direct contact with water. Normally, ½-in. wallboard is used on 16-in. center applications, and ⅝-in. wallboard is used on 24-in. centers. (On 24-in. centers, ⅝-in. wallboard eliminates the "sags" in ceilings and the "waves" in walls frequently created when ½-in. wallboard is used.) Consider repairing lath and plaster or installing wallboard over it as lath and plaster can create quite a mess when you tear into it.

Countertop substrates. Use plywood with exterior glue (sanded on one side), or medium-density fiberboard (MDF) or high-density fiberboard (HDF), as substrates for laminate countertops. Both forms of particleboard, plywood and MDF or HDF, are recommended under plastic laminate, but no form of particleboard is

Use cement board as a backer in a tiled tub/shower area. It's also great on a floor, especially if you're installing radiant heat. The cement board will help to radiate heat into the room.

recommended for use under ceramic, quarry, or mosaic tiles.

Tile. Quarry or mosaic tiles work well for floors and countertops, but ceramic tile is too soft; it may crack if a heavy object is dropped on it. Ceramic tile is, however, good for walls and ceilings, such as tub/shower enclosures and back splashes. At your local home center you can buy marble floor tiles, stone look-alike tiles, and other types of floor and wall tiles.

Wood flooring. Wood floors (engineered or laminated, not solid) work well in a bathroom, but I do not recommend their use directly in front of a bathtub, shower, or any place where they will be in direct contact with water. You can, however, combine wooden flooring with tile for these water-prone areas. Engineered "hardwood" flooring, available both finished and unfinished, is a stable product and does not expand or contract the way lumber and solids do under varying humidity conditions. You may also want to consider the laminated floors manufactured to look like wood. Both engineered and laminated flooring products will work well in a bathroom setting, again, provided they are not in direct contact with water. Contact the manufacturers for more information about the installation of these products in a wet environment, and be sure to read the warranties carefully.

Sheet goods. Resilient, or vinyl, floors are popular for a reason: They're easy to install and easy to maintain. The two kinds of resilient floor coverings, tiles and sheet goods, are explained in greater detail in Chapter Six.

By now I hope you have a realistic assessment of what you want to do and what it will take to accomplish it. Time taken now to make careful plans and material selections is time well spent.

Our dream bathroom required a complete tear-out, even though it was expensive.

The extra effort and cost resulted in this beautiful and functional bathroom.

Demolition and

CHAPTER TWO

Framing

There's a fine art to demolition; it's more than walking into your bathroom with a big hammer and swinging away. To do it right, draw up a game plan and follow it. Start by mentally dissecting your project and putting it back together, as if it were a puzzle. By removing only what you must remove to get your job done, you save on material expenses and avoid unnecessary work.

Safety is a big factor when the dust is flying. When you're doing the demolition work, wear appropriate clothing and protective gear. It's also important, when plumbing and electrical fixtures are involved, that you turn off the water supply and the electrical breakers feeding the fixtures.

Once you've finished gutting, you'll be able to tackle framing, the foundation of any room. The framing will affect everything from the tub to the towel racks, so make sure you take the time to consider exactly how you want your finished project to look.

PRO TIP

In the demolition phase, work slowly and remove a little at a time. It's far easier to make another cut than to repair or replace mistakes.

IN DETAIL

The backing material for older sheet vinyl flooring may contain asbestos. To obtain a sample for testing, carefully cut out a patch with a utility knife and send it to a lab for evaluation. Locate a laboratory in the Yellow Pages of your phone book under "Laboratories-Analytical" or "Asbestos Consulting & Testing." Don't drill, scrape, sand, or cut further into the material until you're sure it's safe. If you do have asbestos in your bathroom, I strongly recommend that you hire a trained, certified removal contractor. Don't track debris containing asbestos into your home; don't do anything that will set the fibers airborne.

WHAT CAN GO WRONG

It's not uncommon for T-bolts, which secure the toilet to the floor, to be so rusted that they're impossible to unscrew. If this is the case with your toilet's T-bolts, cut them off with a minihacksaw.

With the subfloor exposed it's easy to see water damage, which appears to have extended to boards used in construction of the foundation.

Anatomy of a Floor

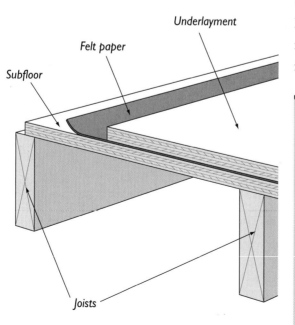

Gutting the Room Completely

Gutting the room is my favorite part of the job. Doors, window frames, plumbing fixtures, underlayment, and subfloor—everything goes. With the framing members exposed, there are no mysteries.

In most of the 5-ft. by 9-ft. bathrooms I remodel, I find two common problems: The existing layout no longer suits the owners, and there's been water damage—mildew, mold, and rot. After gutting I have the opportunity to repair, replace, or reroute any framing members, wiring, ductwork, or plumbing pipes in order to address these issues. And because the room is relatively small, a tear-out is pretty manageable when I'm working alone.

Have a clear picture in your mind (and on paper) of the steps you need to take as you gut and rebuild. Questions that came up during the design-planning phase will be easily answered in the sections below.

Removing floor covering and underlayment

Remove flooring with its underlayment to minimize airborne asbestos fibers. Do not remove flooring and reuse the underlayment. The flooring

+ SAFETY FIRST

Demolition requires that you take some extra measures to protect yourself from injuries: Wear safety goggles, hearing protection, gloves, hardhat, mask or respirator, and work clothes (including boots). I prefer a boot with a high-impact plastic toe versus a steel toe. Instead of using a disposable mask, invest in a respirator; you can purchase different filter cartridges for it to suit the type of work you are doing.

separates from its backing, and it's hard to remove backing and adhesive from the underlayment. New underlayment helps ensure a quality floor installation. Many remodelers lay underlayment over existing flooring, also not a good idea. It creates a height difference at the bathroom doorway and requires adjustments to the door. The toilet flange may also need adjustment.

As for tile, you'll have to remove areas where you can cut into the underlayment so you can remove the flooring in sections. This requires breaking tile with a hammer so be sure to wear eye protection, a long-sleeved shirt, and long pants.

The most manageable, efficient way to remove flooring and underlayment is to cut both layers out as a unit. If your old floor contains asbestos (see "In Detail" on the facing page), this may also be the safest way. Begin the process by removing the toilet, base moldings, any metal threshold molding, and door casings.

Pulling out the toilet. Start by turning off the water supply to the toilet tank and flush the toilet. Use a sponge to absorb any water remaining in the tank and bowl, and then disconnect the water supply to the tank. Pry off the finish caps covering the nuts and T-bolts that secure the toilet to the floor. Unscrew the T-bolt nuts and rock the bowl from side to side to break the seal between the toilet and wax ring. Now twist the bowl and lift straight up. Stow the toilet in a safe place, unless you plan to put in a new one.

Prying off base moldings. Insert a stiff putty knife between the wall and one end of the base molding and pry the molding away from the wall. Once a small section is loose, grab that end and pull. If you plan to save your walls, it is important that you pull the molding down toward the floor; otherwise, the adhesive might tear off the wallboard surface. Rubber or vinyl base moldings are generally not salvageable; you'll need to

Make sure the water does indeed turn off completely; if it doesn't, turn off the main water supply and change the shut-off valve to the toilet.

Pry rubber, vinyl, and wood base molding from the wall using a stiff putty knife.

+ SAFETY FIRST

Be prepared for the unexpected when demolishing a ceiling, especially a lath and plaster one. Ceiling material often comes down quickly and in larger-than-expected chunks, so be sure to wear safety goggles and a hardhat.

TRADE SECRET

If a new tub is not in your plan, cover your current one with a molded plastic protector to prevent falling tiles or dropped tools from marring the surface. Cardboard and painter's tarps also work well.

IN DETAIL

A tub with a scratched or marred surface doesn't have to be replaced. Refinish it or have an acrylic tub liner professionally installed over it. Be sure to check references to determine the quality of the person's work. Refinishing or lining the tub might only be a temporary solution, but either option will lower costs and minimize downtime.

After cutting along the edge of the door casing with a utility knife, use a flat pry bar to help remove the casing from the wall; take care not to damage the casing and/or the lath and plaster wall.

Protecting Doorjambs and Casings
These cuts in the underlayment protect the doorjambs and casings while the rest of the underlayment is removed.

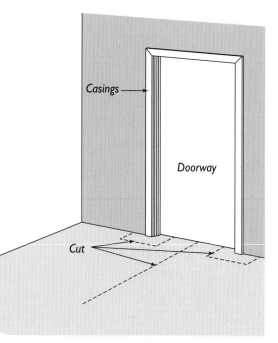

Casings

Doorway

Cut

Use only a utility knife to cut out a sample of floor covering for asbestos testing.

install new ones. Finally, unscrew or pry up the threshold molding between the doorjambs.

Detaching wooden door moldings. If you simply rip the moldings off the wall or door casing, you may damage the wall and the trim. Use a utility knife to cut through any caulk or paint that covers the joint. Always start with the header piece. After the caulk or paint is cut, use a flat pry bar or a small crowbar to carefully detach the rest of the molding.

The underlayment. It is much easier and less complicated to remove the underlayment and flooring as a single unit in manageable increments. The following removal procedure works with a tile floor as well. You may encounter multiple layers of floor covering and underlayment attached with nails and screws. Screws make underlayment especially difficult to remove.

There is a trick to removing underlayment with attached finish flooring. If your bathroom is

Taking up this floor required removing two layers of underlayment and finish floor coverings, a difficult and messy job, in order to reach the subfloor.

Chipping Away at Tile

Before you start, put on your safety goggles to protect your eyes from flying shards of tile. Then break a tile with your hammer and pry it up with a flat pry bar. Break and pry up a few more tiles. A cold chisel works for more stubborn ones. I recommend removing at least a 12-in. by 12-in. area of tile so you can determine the type of underlayment—cement board, plywood or concrete.

If you find cement board or a wood underlayment, remove tiles wherever you'll be cutting the underlayment. If you find concrete, remove the rest of the tiles. Scrape off any remaining adhesive or chisel off the thin-set mortar from the underlayment. After removing the underlayment, you may discover that sections of the subfloor are damaged. In most cases, you can patch in a repair rather than replace the entire subfloor.

Removing existing tile from the tub/shower surround

If your plans call for a new tub/shower surround, you'll need to remove the existing enclosure. In my bathroom, I removed a tile surround. The simple and quick procedure that follows applies just as well to surrounds of vinyl, fiberglass, laminate, and cultured (man-made) stone.

First cut: removing the tub/shower surround. To remove the tub/shower surround, you need to disassemble the plumbing, trim pieces, the casing around the window (if there is one), and the shower rod or door. Use a keyhole wallboard saw to cut through the wall surface and along the edge of the tile or enclosure material. A reciprocating saw will speed up the process, but don't use one if you have lath and plaster walls, especially in adjoining rooms; vibrations will damage them. When you reach a stud, either tip the saw blade so you skim the surface of the stud as you cut the wallboard, or pull the blade out of the wall and reinsert it about 2 in. farther along, bypassing the stud completely. You can then go back and cut those areas by hand. Remove the wallboard and the shower wall material as one unit and discard.

5 ft. by 9 ft., a typical (small) size, remove the vanity cabinet, if possible, to avoid cutting around it and for some working room. Next, use a circular saw to cut around the toilet flange, leaving a 2-in. margin. Set the blade to match the thickness of the layers (the underlayment alone is normally ⅜ in. to ¾ in. thick), so you don't cut through the subfloor. Screws make underlayment especially difficult to remove, so be sure to use a saw blade that will cut through the nails or screws you encounter.

Then make cuts in the center of the doorway and around all the door casings. These cuts allow you to remove the flooring and underlayment without damaging doorjambs and casings. Finally, insert a crowbar into the cuts to pry up the individual sections.

WHAT CAN GO WRONG

Lath and plaster removal is dusty work; wear a respirator and ventilate the area. Shut off the furnace, and then seal cold air returns and heat registers. If you leave the furnace on during this demolition phase, it will suck up dust, clog the filters, and distribute dust throughout the home. Should this happen, turn the furnace off, remove the filters, vacuum the filter area thoroughly, and install new filters. Also seal off doorways to other rooms. Consider renting a ventilation blower to exhaust dust outdoors.

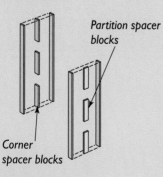

Partition spacer blocks

Corner spacer blocks

TRADE SECRET

During framing save all 12- to 16- in.-long 2×4s to use as the centers when you prebuild corners and partitions. There is no reason to cut up a full-length stud when scraps will be left over from the framing.

Removing Tile Enclosure

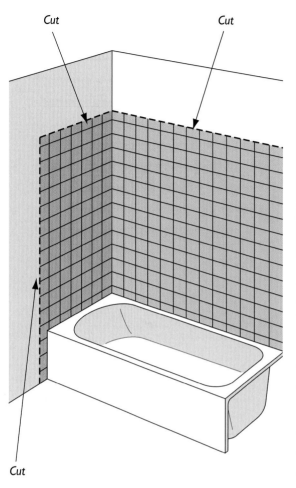

Cut   *Cut*

Cut

Cutting around the perimeter of the tile reduces the mess and allows you to remove a large section of wallboard and tile.

After these walls are open, you may discover that there are no studs near the outside corners of the tub. If this is the case, remove wallboard to the closest studs by cutting horizontally on both ends of the tub starting at the top of the tub/shower enclosure where you previously cut. Then cut vertically to the floor.

Use a Light Touch on Lath and Plaster

If your walls are lath and plaster, you certainly don't want to remove them by swinging a hammer or using a reciprocating saw. The vibration from both these techniques will cause cracks in the finish wall attached to other sides of the studs. Handwork will preserve the wall surface. Use a masonry bit to drill a series of holes in the wall to the depth of the plaster thickness in a 2-in. by 2-in. area near the ceiling. With the claw of a hammer, peel the plaster from the lath in the drilled area. It will be a slow and tedious process but well worth the time invested. After the plaster has been removed and the room has been cleaned up—with your gloves still on—remove the lath from the

The lath and plaster took more time and effort to remove but revealed a false ceiling and more height to work with.

studs. Once this step has been completed, you will be able to see the skeleton, or framework, of the interior walls and address any framing issues.

Windows in showers don't work—as you can see by the water damage to the wall. The newer framed area shows where the window was once located.

Framing

Depending on the extent of your project plans, you'll be faced with different framing techniques and challenges, which could include relocating a wall or door, installing a window, creating a plumbing pocket, repairing floor joists, installing beams and headers, or just framing for a recessed medicine cabinet. The simplest projects involve putting in nailers for towel racks and soap dishes. For my bath, I relocated the door, framed a new smaller window, and added backers for my whirlpool-type tub and custom-made medicine cabinet.

Windows

From experience, I've found that windows installed in the tub/shower area only allow water and moisture to enter the wall, causing mold, mildew, or rot. If possible, eliminate this window. A fan will be required if you remove the only existing vented window.

Tips on Corners and Partitions

Before you start finish-framing, here are a couple of tips to help you frame a corner or a partition (an interior dividing wall). A 2×4 or 2×6 corner consists of the following parts, all nailed together: two studs with three 12-in.- to 16-in.-long 2×4 or 2×6 spacer blocks placed flat between the studs (one at either end and the third one in the center). When it is complete, it should measure 4½ in. wide.

The same is true for a partition, with the exception that the inside blocks (or a full 2×4 or 2×6 to create a "solid partition") are turned sideways (the 3½-in. or 5½-in. way) for a total width of 6½ or 8½ in. when constructed. The turned 2×4 or 2×6 can accept a new wall nailed into it.

If you use a solid partition as a corner, make sure the wall enclosing the tub/shower extends at least 2 in. beyond its edge to allow for the installation of wallboard corner bead and base molding. This solid partition can also provide secure backing for a shower door, as it does in the photo at right.

A backer board nailed to the partition provides framing for the shower pan.

+ SAFETY FIRST

If you want to add or remove a second-floor window, do all the work you can from the inside of the home. You could work from a ladder to repair the exterior side, but it's best to think "safety" and rent scaffolding or a scissors lift from your local rental yard. You'll appreciate the security of having your feet planted on a platform rather than a ladder rung.

TRADE SECRET

If your DWV, dryer vent, or heating ducts run perpendicular to the floor joists and you are unable to hang them below the floor because of restricted ceiling height, create a pocket up in the floor joists to house them. Depending on the pocket's length, you will need either temporary walls or vertical studs to support the joists on both sides while you cut out joist sections for the pocket. Now construct two double cross members from joist material (the same dimension—height and width—as your current joists) to fit up and in between the cut joists. Use joist hangers as shown in the drawing below. You may be required by code to double up the two end joists that support the double cross members. Finally, remove temporary bracing.

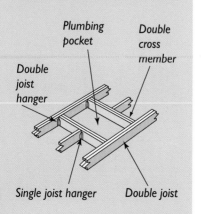

Plumbing pocket

Double cross member

Double joist hanger

Single joist hanger   Double joist

Rough Window Opening

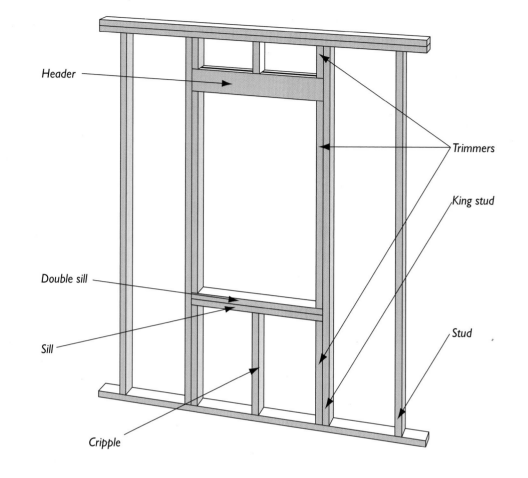

Header

Trimmers

King stud

Double sill

Stud

Sill

Cripple

Removal and enclosing a window. Before removing a window, familiarize yourself with the framing parts of a rough window opening by studying the diagram above. For a wooden window, start by removing all the interior and exterior trim pieces. Look for nails in the vertical parts of the frame and in the sill and stool of the window. Insert a hacksaw blade or metal handsaw between the trimmers (wall framing members) and the wooden window frame, and cut the nails. Then saw between the windowsill (in older windows) and the sill of the framing to cut through the nails, and pull the window into the room. If you want to close in a window opening, follow this step-by-step sequence:

- Nail in the top plate and the bottom plate.
- Measure for the inside trimmers and center stud(s) if necessary, cut them, and nail them in place.
- Install exterior material: sheathing, felt, and matching siding.

Remember to insulate this space after installing any electrical wiring and plumbing but before hanging the wallboard. Incidentally, this same method applies when closing in an existing door.

Doors

It's more likely that you'll just be replacing the door in your remodel, rather than moving the doorway—a step I discuss in depth in Chapter Eight. If you're more ambitious and plan to change the configuration of your space, chances are you'll need to know how to frame a rough opening for a door (see the drawing below). A completed rough door opening frame consists of two king studs, the header, and the bottom plate—all nailed together. To calculate the proper width of the rough open-

**Specifications for Framing
a 30-in. Prehung Rough Door Opening**

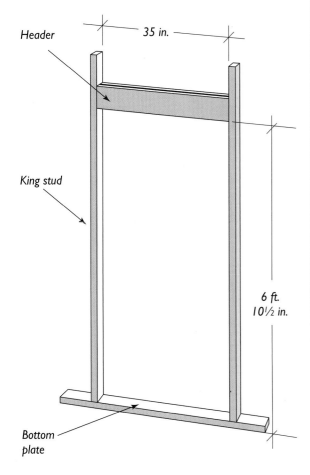

Header

35 in.

King stud

6 ft.
10½ in.

Bottom plate

Boxing the Window

Framing the rough opening for a window can be done from the interior or the exterior side of the house; however, you may find it easier to work from the interior. Construct the rough opening in pieces: first the two king studs, the upper trimmers, the header, and the cripples (if needed). Next, install lower trimmers, the sill, and cripples (if needed). Finally, install the two side trimmers to support the headers. Now cut around the finished rough opening using a reciprocating saw to remove the exterior sheathing. Before you set in the window, cut back the siding to allow room for the window's nailing fin and finish trim.

This pneumatic gun securely nails two plywood trimmers. The header was cut to fit in between two pre-existing studs.

A shim at the sill of an outside corner of the window frame can help to vertically square a window in an out-of-square rough opening. You'll need a helper on the inside to accomplish this. Here the acrylic block window by Hy-Lite is nailed in place using roofing nails through the nailing fin.

TRADE SECRET

If you live in an older home, the trim around exterior and interior windows and doors may not be easily or affordably replaced. Take time to carefully remove and save all trim; you might need it if you damage a piece or later decide to install a new window or door. If you have multiple layers of paint, use a utility knife to cut through it where the trim meets the wall or siding and where the trim meets jambs. Using a skinny nailset to punch the nail through the trim will cause less damage as the trim is removed. (The nailset may have to be ground down to make it work with the nail size.) Alternatively, carefully pull the nails through the back of the molding with end-cutting pliers.

ing you'll need, measure the width of the door plus its frame, add a 3-in. allowance for two 1½-in. trimmers, and add another ½ in. for two ¼-in. spaces on the two sides and ½ in. for the top of the frame (to provide space for adjustments and to shim between the trimmer and the doorframe). For example, a 30-in. pre-hung door measures 31½ in. by 6 ft. 10 in. and will require a rough opening measuring 35 in. by 6 ft. 10½ in. After the rough opening is framed, cut out the bottom plate inside it to install the trimmers. After the trimmers are in place, you can install the upper trimmers and center cripple.

It is important that you build the door rough opening frame as one unit and keep the bottom plate in place until the frame is completely installed. This helps to keep the frame straight and aligned. If either of the king studs becomes misaligned, your door will not close properly.

Working on the Floor System

Hopefully, your bathroom floor is in good shape. If you are unable to examine the bathroom floor undercarriage because you do not have access to it or your basement ceiling is finished, then removal of the underlayment, if it's required by your plans, will help you to determine the direction of your floor joists. This is also an opportunity to assess the true condition of your floor. If you discover water or insect damage or need to relocate plumbing to accommodate your design plan, it may be necessary to remove some or all of the subfloor.

Most of the subfloor has been replaced; the toilet area is the only section remaining. The main soil pipe will be moved once the cast-iron pipe is replaced with one made of plastic called ABS (acrylonitrile butadiene styrene).

How to remove the subfloor

The subfloor provides support to your entire room. It's the layer of flooring that is directly attached to the floor joists, and the one to which the underlayment and finish floor are applied. The tub/shower pan and any radiant heating system or cement board you install all sit directly on it.

As a general rule, subfloors don't need replacement unless they have been damaged by water or insects, so if your subfloor is in good shape and moving plumbing fixtures is not in your plan, don't touch it. If you discover damage, replace only the affected areas. Because the subfloor sits directly underneath the wall plates, you will need to cut around the perimeter of the room with a reciprocating saw to remove it. Cut in the center of entryways and around doorjambs using either a reciprocating or a circular saw. Be sure to remove felt paper or nails and screws that have popped up before you begin cutting with a circular saw; they will interfere with it. Set the circular saw at the depth of the subfloor thickness and cut the subfloor into manageable sections. When removing the subfloor, always work from the back wall toward the door entrance. This allows you a solid platform on which to work.

If for any reason you have to remove the subfloor completely—because of water damage, joists that need repairs or support, or if there is not enough room in the crawlspace to work comfortably—install a new subfloor that's at least ¾ in. thick (or as thick as it needs to be to match the level of adjacent subflooring).

Dealing with floor joists

In some cases, the floor will have a crawlspace underneath it, and in other cases the floor may double as a ceiling for a basement. It may be on the second story, in which case it's over a finished ceiling of the living space beneath it. Whatever the circumstances, it's been my experience that

Use plenty of construction adhesive on the tops of the floor joists before installing the subfloor.

Easy Access to Crawlspace

In a crawlspace situation, removing the subfloor allows easy access to the joists to run electrical wires, reconfigure plumbing, or reposition a heating duct along, between, or through the joists.

Taking up the subfloor also gives you a chance to install fiberglass insulation and a vapor barrier. First, cover the ground with 4- or 6-mil black polyethylene as a moisture barrier. Then attach insulation hangers between the joists to hold the insulation in place (face up) while you staple it.

dealing with floor joists can be complicated. When it comes to fishing an electrical wire or installing new plumbing, the joists will run in the wrong direction, or a joist will be located exactly where I need to install some pipes. It just never fails—but with a little knowledge of the joist system, some blessings from the building department, and a reciprocating saw, most problems can be overcome.

PRO TIP

If you invest in a crimper tool, you'll be able to cut your duct pipe to length and then crimp the end to fit.

WHAT CAN GO WRONG

Plumbing supply lines are small enough to run through holes drilled in framing members, but the same can't be said for ductwork. When a run of ductwork has to extend across joists instead of between them, you'll need to re-route the duct or build a soffit to hide it.

The plumbing pocket is completed using joist hangers. Here, ¾-in plywood was fastened with glue and screws to the inside of the left joist to provide extra support where the 2-in. drainpipe passes through the joist.

With auto feed and an extended barrel, this **Quik Drive®** tool makes it easy to screw down the plywood subfloor.

If you discover a floor joist where the drainpipe needs to be located, plan for an opening, or pocket, for that plumbing. If you have to cut a floor joist to create that pocket, then add extra support to the existing joists on both sides of it to shore up the weakened framing member. Joist hangers will help support any joists you've cut and make nailing easier. This pocket can serve as an area through which plumbing, heating ducts, and wiring can run.

When constructing a pocket or channel, build temporary support walls underneath joists to hold them in place while you cut them. (If you need to cut just one joist, then a single 2×4 underneath the joist will provide sufficient support.) Without support, the weight above the joist will put direct pressure on the cut and bind the saw. It will also force the joists to drop out of alignment, making it impossible to install and attach the beam in place. It could also cause structural damage to the walls above it. Be sure to have a couple of hydraulic jacks and two 4×4s on hand to jack the beam up and hold it in place while you secure the joist hangers. When installing the temporary sup-

✚ SAFETY FIRST

Exposed joists are dangerous, so do everything you can to prevent accidents. Be sure to cover any openings in the floor with plywood. If you have small children, consider installing key locks on all doors that access the construction area.

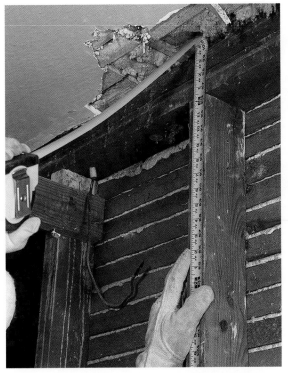

Expect surprises when you expose old framing. In this remodel, we discovered a false ceiling with joists that had simply been nailed to studs instead of supported by a ledger board.

Even if the pipe is purchased pre-crimped, you may still need to use a crimper tool to achieve a good fit.

port wall, leave yourself enough room to work comfortably.

Working on the Venting

The proper venting of a bathroom exhaust fan—and its associated ductwork—is often ignored. Because it's so difficult to install these items in a ceiling that isn't open, take advantage of exposed ceiling and floor joists to conceal ductwork or open the ceiling.

Venting ductwork

Now, while everything is open, evaluate your current exhaust fan to see that it has an adequate cfm rating to properly vent the square footage of your bathroom. It's also a good time to upgrade or replace your existing fan. Perhaps you want to add extra heat; you'll want to consider a heat/fan/light unit. All such units require proper venting to the outside of the house, not just into your attic.

Use 4-in. aluminum pipe for bathroom fans if the runs are horizontal. You'll also need adjustable elbows, metal duct tape, a five-blade crimper, and aviation snips. A 2×4 nailed to the underside between two joists will support the weight of the pipe and prevent it from sagging (and possibly separating at the joints), especially if it is installed over a lengthy run. Secure the ductwork to a framing member with a plumbing strap to keep the pipe as straight as possible.

✓ According to Code

The maximum run with rigid ductwork is a 14-ft. combined horizontal and vertical length, which includes two 90-degree elbows. For each additional elbow, deduct 2 ft. from the overall length of your pipe. Check the manufacturer's guidelines, though, because they supersede code requirements.

PRO TIP

As a precaution, hold the side handle on the 1/2-in. electric drill for better control and to prevent the drill from twisting out of your hands.

TRADE SECRET

If your soil pipe extends slightly beyond your stud wall, it will prevent you from installing your wallboard flat against the studs. Instead of bending wallboard over the pipe, cut furring strips the same width as the framing members—this is easily done with a table saw—and nail them to the studs. The wallboard will then clear the soil pipe.

For lath-and-plaster walls, fasten furring strips to the face of the framing members using either screws or a pneumatic finish nailer.

An angle drill with an extra long bit helps to drill a pilot hole to the outside when the rim joist is set back.

Bathroom fan ductwork should be seamed with metal duct tape, which will fuse the pipe together. Do not use cloth tape because it can dry out and fall off over time. You must not fasten the duct sections together with screws; this will allow moisture from the bathroom fan to leak at the screw holes.

The damper system requires a 4¼-in. hole (¼ in. larger than the 4-in. standard pipe) through the rim joist to the exterior of the building or up through the roof. Use a hole saw for the exterior of the building (the option I prefer) or a reciprocating saw for the roof. Begin by drilling a pilot hole through the center of the backside of the rim joist or roof sheathing. Drill all the way through using a 3/16-in. or smaller bit. If you encounter any obstacles at this point, repairing the small hole is easy.

With the pilot hole drilled, you can now drill from the exterior surface, placing the hole saw in the previously drilled pilot hole. After the hole is cut, it's time to trial-fit your damper installation. Once you feel comfortable with the fit, remove the damper, apply latex caulk to the backside of the damper hood, and attach the unit. Damper hoods come with two or four predrilled holes. If yours only has two holes, drill two more holes in the outside corners. Attach the damper using galvanized or stainless-steel screws, not nails.

After you install the damper and before connecting the pipe, it is a good idea to install the plastic flange plate (ring) that comes with the damper kit. First apply latex caulk on the inside of the flange plate and around the damper pipe to prevent moisture and cold air from entering the home. Then mount the flange plate, pushing the flange into the caulk up against the backside of the rim joist or the underside of the roof sheathing.

After the screws are installed, check to make sure the damper door opens and closes freely.

Other Framing Projects

Don't forget to frame for a recessed medicine cabinet if one's included in your plan. Just as in framing for a window, you'll need to know the measurements of your rough opening. If you plan to install the medicine cabinet on a bearing wall, the structure of your roof above it might require that you use a header. Some early plumbing will be required at this framing stage, such as installing the drain/overflow and fitting the tub/shower into place.

Here are some other points to consider when framing:

- Allow for backing support, such as a nailer, for a wall-hung washbasin or toilet, showerhead, rafter corners (where the ceiling meets the wall), grab bars, and mirrors.
- An extra 2×4 to support the light box allows you to install your light fixture independent of the medicine cabinet.

Backer boards are installed to provide a solid fastening foundation for our custom-made wall cabinet.

Backer Board for Ceiling Installation

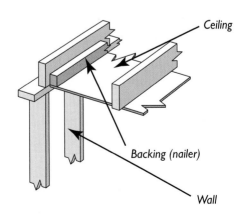

Ceiling

Backing (nailer)

Wall

If you plan to install a built-in heater, trial-fit the unit to make sure the framing will accommodate both it and the wiring.

TRADE SECRET

You don't have to install the entire subfloor before you install the tub—lay only the subfloor the tub will sit on to the nearest joist outside the width of the tub. Apply construction adhesive to the joists, and then secure the subfloor with screws to hold the floor system together and minimize squeaks. You can then repair or replace the remaining subfloor after the tub has been installed.

WHAT CAN GO WRONG

If you plan to install a window close to the ceiling line to let a little extra light into a shower area, you'll need to use a header. It's a good idea to open both the wall and the ceiling in this area to see if you have the space for a header, otherwise you will have to lower the window. Also, take into consideration that the roof overhang and soffit, normally lower than the interior ceiling height, can restrict window light.

The stud closest to the tub is a nailer for wallboard. The middle stud serves as a nailer for the tub and, together with the third stud, for the shower door.

- A steel bathtub requires adequate support at the back wall. (Cast-iron tubs do not because, unlike steel tubs, they are not flexible.) Read the manufacturer's instructions.
- The rim of a whirlpool-type tub is not designed to carry the weight of any finish material, such as tile or cultured marble, that comes in contact with or rests on it. Again, read the instructions supplied with the unit.

✓ According to Code

Remember that city, county, or state inspectors for electrical, plumbing, and construction will have to inspect and approve different phases of the job, so make sure you know the inspection schedule before you cover any of the work with finish materials.

- Attach a 2×4 against the stud to serve as a nailer for new wallboard material. You'll also need support for a shower door. If you're planning to use one, install a 2×4 or 2×6 about 3 in. in from the edge of the tub/shower.
- You might have to put down a second subfloor in your bathroom as a "filler" to match the level of existing adjoining floors in your home. It's also important to securely screw down the existing subfloor. Be sure to put felt paper between the layers and use screws—not nails— to prevent any squeaks.

Finishing Up the Framing

The final step in framing isn't really framing at all— it's setting the tub. This is a good time to do it, especially if you have no storage for the tub or you have a single-bathroom home and need the facilities. This might sound like an easy job, but keep in mind that a 5-ft. standard or whirlpool-type tub installed in a 5-ft.-wide bathroom can make for a tight fit. Setting the tub requires installing the waste drain and overflow on the tub, attaching support on the back wall for the back rim of the tub, and cutting the subfloor to accept the drain and overflow. Any corrections to framing should be made now to ensure that the tub fits and that the plumbing won't interfere with any of the framing members.

The photos on the facing page provide an outline to help you hook up the combination waste and overflow (required before you can install your tub), cut out the subfloor to accommodate the drain, and hook up the P-trap. The diagrams and the information under "Bathtub measurements" in Chapter Three will prove helpful here. Be sure to follow any instructions your manufacturer may have provided for your particular unit.

Now that the framing is complete and the tub is in, it's time to move on to rough-in plumbing.

FRAMING FOR THE TUB

Begin this final framing work by fitting the overflow to the back (through the upper hole) and attaching the retainer plate. Next, connect the waste elbow (follow manufacturer's instructions) and the waste flange. A tub drain wrench will be helpful to tighten the waste flange.

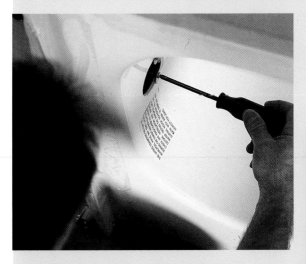

Temporarily tighten all the nuts to the waste and overflow tubes. After the system is hooked up, examine the waste and overflow configuration to roughly determine how much subfloor to cut out.

Using a jigsaw in a plunge mode, I am cutting the subfloor to accommodate the tub waste and overflow drain. Normally, a bathtub requires an access hole in the subfloor that is 6 in. wide and extends out 12 in. from the plumbing wall; the 6 in. measurement begins 12 in. out from the sidewall. But your tub, like ours, may have a different plumbing configuration and require a larger access hole (see the photo at right).

Quite a bit of subfloor had to be removed to accommodate the combination waste and overflow drain, P-trap, and vent for this whirlpool-type tub. This photo also illustrates how the P-trap is connected to the overflow drain. Even if you didn't have to disturb your main plumbing drain and you put in a new tub, I recommend that you replace the P-trap with a new unit for a no-leak installation.

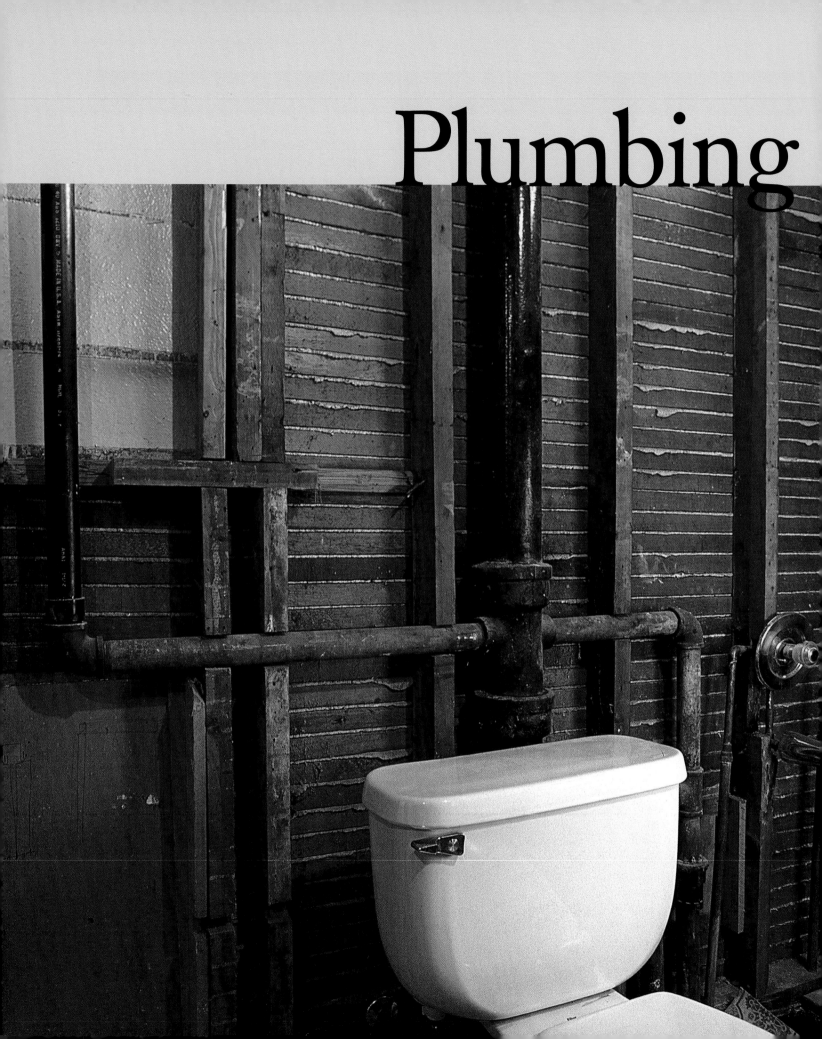

Plumbing

CHAPTER THREE
Rough-In

A ll that remains of my old bathroom is the toilet and a network of pipes, drains, and vents. My plans call for relocating the vanity, moving the toilet, and installing a new tub. With open walls, I can see what's involved in replacing my 56-year-old system.

Your bathroom's skeleton will also be exposed, which makes it easy to see where and how waste, supply, and vent lines should run. Study it carefully and consider how each upgrade affects the plumbing. If you're moving the toilet, for example, you'll need to relocate the soil pipe and the supply line. You may have to redesign the venting system to accommodate the new drains.

This chapter introduces you to the basics. You'll need to consider different scenarios and familiarize yourself with the pipes and fittings. Study the drawings carefully; they provide key elements to help you design and install a plumbing system that meets code.

PRO TIP

If this is your first rough-in plumbing project, consider hiring a plumbing contractor as a consultant.

IN DETAIL

Wastewater and sewage are removed from your home through a network of independent drains leading from each fixture to a main large-diameter soil pipe (the "main stack") that eventually leads out of the house to a sewer or septic tank. The branch drains and waste pipes use gravity; the code requires specific down-ward slopes for steady flow. This drainage system requires prop-erly designed vents to work effectively. Upward sloping vents prevent siphoning and keep each fixture's trap ("P-trap") filled with water to keep sewer gases from entering the home.

Typical Three-Piece Bathroom DWV System

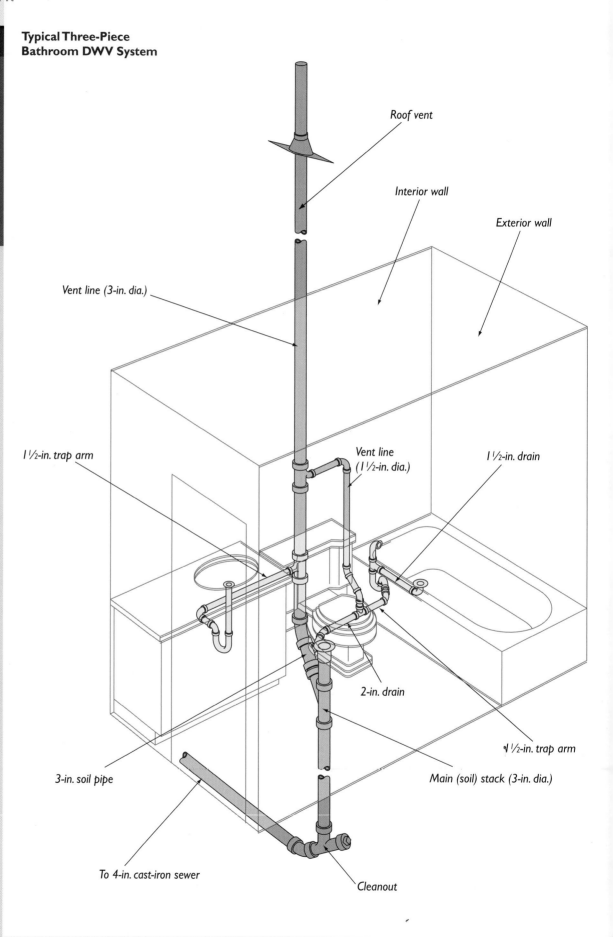

Roof vent

Interior wall

Exterior wall

Vent line (3-in. dia.)

1½-in. trap arm

Vent line (1½-in. dia.)

1½-in. drain

2-in. drain

1½-in. trap arm

3-in. soil pipe

Main (soil) stack (3-in. dia.)

To 4-in. cast-iron sewer

Cleanout

Learning Plumbing Basics

The plumbing components of a typical three-fixture bathroom are the drain, waste, and vent (DWV) system and the water supply system. A home that hasn't been remodeled should retain its original basic plumbing anatomy, but if the bath has been renovated, it may deviate from current plumbing codes. While the walls are exposed, inspect the plumbing layout. Once you're familiar with it, you'll be better equipped to make the required changes and handle unexpected problems. This chapter will give you a better understanding of a working DWV system. Your design may not be identical to this, but the drawing on the facing page identifies basic layout and component details.

If you have a standard 5-ft. by 9-ft. bathroom, you may find that there are very few ways to lay it

Standard Rough Plumbing Layout for a Three-Fixture Bathroom Setting

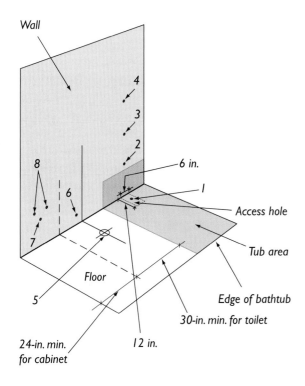

out. Local codes usually dictate a maximum distance between plumbing fixtures and the main stack. Because tubs are as wide as the room, they're usually placed in a corner perpendicular to the plumbing wall. The washbasin and toilet are located on the plumbing wall in the remaining space between the tub and the room door. You may want to locate the vanity to take advantage of natural light from a window or skylight. Of course, you probably considered these ideas in Chapter One, but you should keep them in mind as you continue to hone your plan.

Laying Out the Fixture Rough-In

The rough-in layout for a three-fixture bathroom is pretty basic. Before you can begin, take note of the standard measurements in the drawing at left. These measurements are always given as "dead center." Remember that when you're measuring from rough framing you must allow for the thickness of the finished wall. The following recommendations—and those given throughout this book—are by no means the final word on the subject. Be sure to follow local building and plumbing codes.

Bathtub measurements

The following measurements are based on a standard 30-in.-wide bathtub. If you have a wider tub or a whirlpool-type tub like mine, the drain will be centered on the tub's width. This is where it's helpful to have fixtures on hand and a complete floor plan. Measure the fixtures more than once to make sure you have the right dimensions.

1. The bathtub drain in the floor is 3 in. below the finish floor level and 1½ in. from the rough plumbing wall. It's centered in a 30-in. space, the width of the bathtub. Cut a 6-in. by 12-in. access

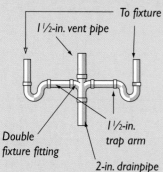

To fixture

1 ½-in. vent pipe

Double fixture fitting

1 ½-in. trap arm

2-in. drainpipe

Double sanitary tee
(Not a code-compliant fixture fitting.)

Double fixture tee
(A code-compliant fixture fitting.)

IN DETAIL

If you're installing side-by-side (dual) or back-to-back wash-basins, make sure you use the correct fittings. The trap arms and vent pipe are 1½ in.; the drain, however, is 2 in. In either case, install a cleanout fitting below the shared drain. Do not use a double sanitary tee—it's a venting fitting and is not code-compliant in this situation. Instead, use a double fixture tee. Check out the illustration above to see the difference between the two fittings and how the correct one is used.

The plumbing pocket accommodates the P-trap, trap arm, and vent for the Jacuzzi's waste and overflow drain.

hole in the subfloor, 12 in. in from the sidewall, for the waste and overflow drains. If you are installing a shower, use the actual shower pan as a guide to correctly locate the drain.

2. The tub spout is located 5 in. above the top edge of the bathtub.

3. The tub faucet is 10 in. to 12 in. above the top edge of the bathtub. In a shower stall, the shower faucet should be 48 in. from the finish floor.

4. The showerhead is located roughly 6 ft. 2 in. from the bottom of the tub.

Toilet measurements

The type of toilet you plan to install—wall-hung or a standard floor model—will make a difference in where you place the rough-in plumbing. For a wall-hung toilet, you'll have to consider if you need additional support, such as a nailer or backer board. The drawing on p. 43 reflects a standard floor model.

5. The toilet drain is 12½ in. from the center to the rough framing and is centered in a minimum of 30 in. of finished space. Again, this assumes ½-in. wallboard. If you're installing wall tile, add the thickness of the tile and mastic to

As a general rule, set the toilet flange 12½ in. (on center) from the unfinished wall. This measurement accommodates the thickness of the wallboard.

the 12½-in. measurement. With a specialized toilet, be sure to check the installation instructions.

6. The water supply is located 6 in. up from the finish floor and is 6 in. to the left of the center of the toilet drain as you face the wall. Bring the water supply line out 5 in. to 6 in. from the rough framing. It will be cut off later when it is time to install the shutoff valve.

Washbasin measurements

Once you have established the height and width of your cabinet, you can determine where to locate the drain. In the drawing on p. 43 and the top photo at right, the drain is centered in the minimum 24-in. space required for a washbasin. Smaller cabinets and washbasins are available if you don't have this much space.

7. The washbasin drain is 18 in. to 20 in. above the finish floor, depending on the height of the cabinet, and is centered in a minimum of 24 in. of cabinet space.

8. The water supply lines—hot to the left and cold to the right—are 4 in. to the left and right of the drain. Bring the lines out 5 in. to 6 in. from the rough framing (they will be cut off later when shutoff valves are installed), and 22 in. to 24 in. off the finish floor, depending upon the height of the cabinet.

Working with Plastic Pipes and Fittings

Most homes today contain DWV systems constructed of ABS or polyvinyl chloride (PVC)—both cost-effective and easy to work with—as opposed to copper, galvanized steel, or cast-iron branches and waste lines. For that reason, I'm going to focus on ABS and PVC.

To support the cold water line, a backer board was installed to accommodate the pipe clamps. It took two different clamp styles to securely hold the pipe in place.

Your DWV system will be made up of these different types of pipes. A: Copper; B: Schedule 40 PVC; C: Galvanized; D: Schedule 40 ABS Drain/vent pipe; E: Cast iron

✔ According to Code

Plastic pipe might seem to be an easy plumbing solution, but check with your building department to ensure that the product you plan to use meets code, especially for water supply lines. PVC water-supply piping is generally not allowed for interior use. Also, use the appropriate solvent cement; all-purpose solvent cement doesn't meet either the Uniform Plumbing Code (UPC) or International Plumbing Code (IPC).

IN DETAIL

Cutting a vertical soil pipe requires two supporting riser clamps—one attached 6 in. to 12 in. above your planned cut, and one 6 in. to 12 in. below it. If you are cutting no more than 12 in. above the floor, install two 2×4 support blocks for the upper riser clamps to rest on. The lower one can rest on the

floor or on the bottom plate. If there are no studs to which you can fasten these support blocks, build a framework around the pipe, allowing room for the soil pipe cutter to fit in and around the pipe. When I cut my soil pipe I didn't need to use supports. The hub of the cast-iron pipe provided support to the upper pipe being cut. When you use the pipe cutter, grasp the handle with one hand and the ratchet wrench with the other. For photographic purposes, I removed my hand from the handle.

Types of plastic pipe

These three types of plastic pipe are used across the country—ABS and chlorinated polyvinyl chloride (CPVC) more commonly in the west and PVC in the east.

ABS (acrylonitrile butadiene styrene). DWV pipe is black and resistant to sewage, household chemicals, and more. It's joined by ABS solvent cement and fittings, and easily connected to galvanized steel, copper, or cast iron with transition fittings.

PVC (polyvinyl chloride). DWV pipe is white and resistant to acids, alkalis, and salt solutions. Like ABS, it's easy to work with and joined by PVC solvent cement and fittings.

CPVC (chlorinated polyvinyl chloride). Usually a yellowish color, CPVC has the same chemical characteristics as PVC but is used for hot and cold water supply lines. It resists heat better than PVC and is joined by CPVC solvent cement and fittings, or by grip fittings.

Drain, waste, and vent parts

Your local home center stocks fittings in various sizes and shapes, which boil down to the following basic parts:

- *45° elbows and 90° long-sweep elbows*—used to make gradual bends in pipe runs.
- *90° elbows*—used to make right-angle bends in pipe runs.

"Prohibited" Fittings

Many municipalities in the United States enforce either one or both of two major codes: the Uniform Plumbing Code (UPC) and the International Plumbing Code (IPC). Work with your plumbing inspector to select plumbing pipes and fittings that are approved by the code in your area. Avoid fittings that are prohibited by the UPC and IPC.

Prohibited Fittings

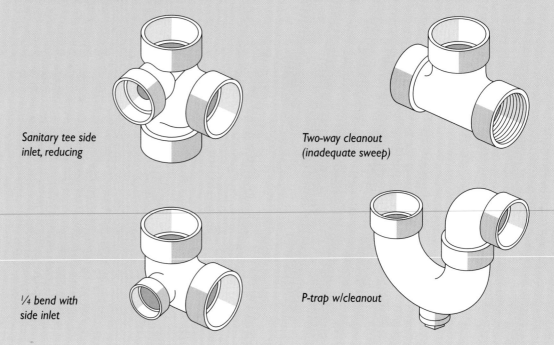

Sanitary tee side inlet, reducing

Two-way cleanout (inadequate sweep)

¼ bend with side inlet

P-trap w/cleanout

- *T-fittings*—used to connect branch lines. Frequently called a "waste T" or a "sanitary T."
- *Y-fittings*—used to join intersecting pipes.
- *couplings*—used to join two straight pipes.
- *reducers*—used to connect pipes of different diameters. Also available in T-fittings and elbows.

Before you proceed to the next section, put your system together without adhesives (a dry fit). Then schedule an inspection to get it approved. Some plumbing inspectors prefer to see an unglued system; if something doesn't meet code requirements you'll be able to correct it with greater ease.

Cutting and joining plastic pipe. It's easy to construct permanent leak-proof joints with ABS and PVC fittings if you follow these rules:

1. **Make square cuts.** Use a miter box, electric miter saw, or a ratchet plastic-tubing cutter. If the end isn't square, the pipe won't seat correctly, creating a weak joint.

2. **Remove burrs and rough edges.** Use a utility knife to remove any burrs on the pipe end—inside and out. Rough edges can scrape away the solvent cement during assembly.

3. **Degloss the surface.** For better adhesion, use emery paper to sand the outside of the pipe and the inside of the fitting. I recommend 3M®'s green finishing pads for plastic and copper. Hold the pad over one end and twist the pipe.

4. **Test the fit.** On a trial run, the pipe should go only halfway into its mate. If the pipe easily bottoms, the fit is too loose and most likely the solvent cement will not form a leak-free joint. Adjust the fit if necessary.

5. **Use alignment marks.** Before taking pipe and fittings apart, draw an alignment mark across each joint. Use a black marker on PVC and a white or yellow one on ABS.

Surfaces to be glued should have a dull finish.

An alignment mark across each joint will assure an exact fit.

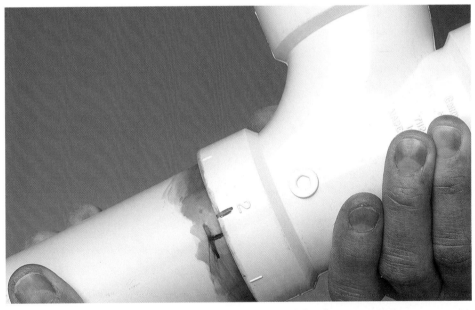

Put the pipe and fitting together off your alignment mark by about a quarter turn. Immediately, before the solvent cement evaporates, twist to the mark to finish.

✛ SAFETY FIRST

Never stand under the work area and look directly up where solvent cement is being applied—either stand off to one side or position yourself above it. Always wear eye protection.

PRO TIP

Cutting off too much metal piping could leave you short when it's time to hook it up with new plastic pipe. Leave existing pipe long, then cut to fit.

IN DETAIL

Check with your building department before drilling a floor joist for drainpipes. In 2×10s or 2×12s you can usually drill holes that are large enough to accept a 2-in. pipe, but the hole must be at least 2 in. away from the top or bottom edge of the joist. Sometimes, after drilling through 2×4s in a wall, not much of the stud remains. Piping that's too close to the edge of a stud could also be penetrated by your wallboard fastener. Stud guards (18-gauge galvanized steel, 1½ in. by 3 in. or 1½ in. by 5 in.) are required by code and can eliminate reopening a wall to repair an accidental puncture.

6. Apply primer (PVC only). Use primer specifically designed for PVC to remove dirt and soften the pipe for a stronger bond. Apply primer first to the inside of the fitting, then to the outside of the pipe. Wait five to fifteen seconds before applying solvent cement.

7. Apply solvent cement. Follow the manufacturer's recommendation for usage on the plastic you're installing. Brush a thin, even coat of cement inside the fitting. Be careful not to apply too much. Next, brush a liberal coat onto the pipe, covering the primer.

8. Assemble immediately. Use enough force to ensure that the pipe bottoms in the fitting socket before the cement evaporates. Give the fitting a quarter turn as you push it in and hold firmly for 30 seconds. Solvent cement chemically fuses the fitting to the pipe, so if your fit is off, cut out the mistake and start over.

9. Look for a continuous bead. If the ring of solvent cement pushed out during assembly doesn't completely surround the joint, you haven't used enough and the joint could leak. Cut out the joint and start over.

10. Remove excess solvent cement. Wipe it off with a clean white rag, leaving an even film all the way around. This helps the joint cure faster. Let sit for at least 30 minutes.

Plumbing challenges

Frequently special fittings are needed to incorporate new plumbing into the existing plumbing.

Working with cast-iron pipe. In my bathroom I had to replace a section of cast-iron drainpipe, which required using a pipe cutter. To do this, I planted all the cutter wheels squarely around the pipe, then tightened the feed screw just enough to make an indentation onto the pipe. Next, I loosened the feed-screw knob slightly, rotated the unit, and retightened. To complete the cut, I made sure the cutter wheels sat in the indentations, then tightened the ratchet.

The Indispensable Pipe Wrench

There is simply no substitute for a good-quality pipe wrench. It's an indispensable plumbing tool and frequently two are needed to remove or tighten galvanized pipe. Originally, pipe wrenches were only made of steel, but today they are available in aluminum, which makes them a lot lighter and easier to manipulate.

To use a pipe wrench, adjust the upper jaw by turning the knurled (ridged) knob and fit the tool over the pipe. Turn the wrench slightly until the teeth bite into the pipe, and apply pressure on the upper movable jaw. The spring-loaded jaw is slightly angled, which allows you to release the grip and reposition the wrench without readjusting the jaw. If you're working overhead, stand on a solidly planted stepladder to achieve the proper leverage and prevent injury if the tool slips. Keep your face away from the tool in case a plumbing part loosens faster than anticipated.

This end pipe wrench permits work on galvanized pipes in restricted spaces or close to a wall.

I tightened the two clamps with a screwdriver, although a ratchet wrench will also work. Be careful not to go too far—you'll break the clamp.

After fitting the replacement ABS pipe up to newly cut cast-iron drainpipe, I removed the ABS pipe and slid a rubber coupling over the cast-iron pipe. Next I butted the ABS pipe up to the cast-iron pipe and pulled the coupling over the ABS so it straddled the ABS and cast-iron pipes equally. Finally, I tightened the clamps.

Finding the drainpipe. The challenge I faced when installing a floor drain for my new hot water tank was to find a drainpipe buried under 4 in. of concrete. I used RIDGID's SeeSnake® diagnostic equipment, which has a camera head attached to the end of the snake and a hand-held pointer receiver. If you know your pipe is cast iron, a metal detector might work instead—just be aware that screening or rebar (reinforcing bar) in the floor might throw you off.

Before inserting the camera head into the drainpipe, I used a blow bag (also known as an expansion nozzle) to clean a plugged drain beneath the concrete floor. Available in a variety of sizes, blow bags use powerful spurts of water to blast clogs away. I attached it to a garden hose,

Rubber Donuts for Use with Cast-Iron Pipe

Sections of cast-iron pipe are held together with packing oakum and hot molten lead, but this joinery method won't work if you need to connect a plastic pipe into the hub of a cast-iron fitting. A rubber ring ("donut") is your solution, but they are not always easy to use.

- After adding lubricant to the ABS pipe, insert it into the donut to form a watertight seal.
- Lubricate the inside of the cast-iron hub and the outside of the donut and then place the donut and pipe into the hub as far as it will go—which is not very far.
- With one end of a 2×4 (about 14-in. long) up against the donut, use a mallet to tap the other end of the 2×4, working it around the donut until the donut is completely into the hub—it will take some force.
- Then with the 2×4 flat across the ABS pipe, use the mallet on the 2×4 to drive the pipe in farther.

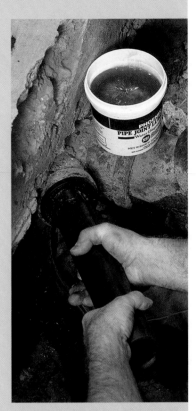

A generous amount of lubricant is required to install pipe into the donut.

A blow bag unclogs drains better than many chemicals do.

49

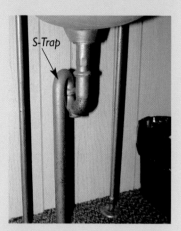

S-Trap

(Photo © Leon A. Frechette)

WHAT CAN GO WRONG

Using a long-radius TY fitting in your vent pipes actually prevents natural venting and recreates the self-siphoning characteristics similar to those of an S-trap, as shown in the photo above. This self-siphoning effect breaks the seal at the crown of the trap so that it drains out, allowing sewer gases into the home. For this reason, S-traps and long-radius TY fittings are no longer code-compliant. Instead, use a sanitary tee that permits venting off the top half of the trap arm and keeps the P-trap sealed.

placed it into the pipe, and turned on the water. While cold water increased the life of the product, hot water did a better job of unclogging the drain. Before using hot water, I started with cold water to make the blow bag seal in the pipe.

Because the main plumbing is going to be redone in this area, I cut and removed an 8-in. section of the 2-in. drainpipe leading into the 4-in. soil pipe. Then I inserted the camera head and viewed the inside of the pipe on the monitor. The pointer receiver picked up signals from a transmitter just behind the camera head and accurately pinpointed the center and depth of the pipe. After marking the floor and protecting the furnace and hot water heater with cardboard, I broke through the concrete floor using an electric breaker hammer (jackhammer).

Installing a cleanout. It's inevitable that drains clog, which is why cleanout valves are

required. A cleanout allows accessibility to the drain or soil pipe to clear an obstruction within the pipe. The challenge is to include a cleanout at the base of the soil pipe that isn't intrusive, either physically or visually, yet meets the codes regarding accessibility. In a bathroom, P-traps act as cleanouts because they can be removed to provide access to the trap arms that lead to the drainpipe.

A cleanout is required on a soil pipe. The minimum clearance in front of this cleanout needs to be 18 in. on soil pipes 3 in. and larger. Cleanouts cannot be concealed, and, if they are built into walls, the wall must have an opening for accessibility. Generally, the main stack cleanout lands in space underneath the bathroom, such as a basement bath or laundry room, or in a crawlspace. If the soil pipe lands in the crawlspace, it must be located within 20 ft. of the crawlspace opening.

This very accessible 3-in. ABS cleanout was installed after replacing all the 4-in. cast-iron pipe to the upstairs bathroom. The drainpipes shown will serve our new bath-laundry in the basement.

This ABS offset flange allows you to mount a new toilet onto old plumbing.

Replacing an older toilet. The challenge in replacing an older toilet is that new toilets sit at 12 in. on center from the finish wall while some older toilets sit at 10 in. or 14 in., usually on cast-iron pipes. If you face this situation, an offset flange might allow you to complete your hookup without removing the entire soil pipe. Offset flanges are available in ABS, PVC, brass, and copper to match up with different types of soil pipes. They're available in a variety of offset sizes. Be sure to measure carefully from the finished wall to the center of the toilet flange for accurate toilet placement and be sure to check code compliance before using.

Installing Vent Piping

Now that we have tackled the drain/waste section, let's look at the other side of the equation: vent piping. Without vent pipes, the drainage system won't work properly. By providing air to the drains, vents permit them to flow freely. If a vent becomes clogged, the pipes won't empty completely. Vents also allow sewer gases to escape to the exterior.

There are two types of venting systems: wet venting and dry venting. A wet venting system uses the drain system of one fixture to vent another fixture. A dry venting system only carries air, i.e., it does not have drainage flowing through it.

Wet venting systems

When creating your DWV system, start with the proper code-compliant fittings. Determine the maximum run, meaning the distance from the vent pipe to the trap arm (technically, from the center of the P-trap back to the center of the vent pipe). The wet venting system illustrated on p. 52 represents a typical three-fixture bathroom.

PRO TIP

Cut a peephole behind base molding to locate vent pipes coming down between floors. Listen for your helper to drop the pipe on the framing plate.

IN DETAIL

To install a new vent pipe, first run a full length down through the roof. Lengthen the pipe by gluing on couplings and seating additional pipes. You'll need a helper—the long pipe will be unmanageable. This is not a windy-day project. Framing plates will prevent you from dropping the pipe to the next level, so drill holes through them to accommodate the diameter of the pipe and/or coupling. You may have to open a wall or ceiling.

Wet Venting

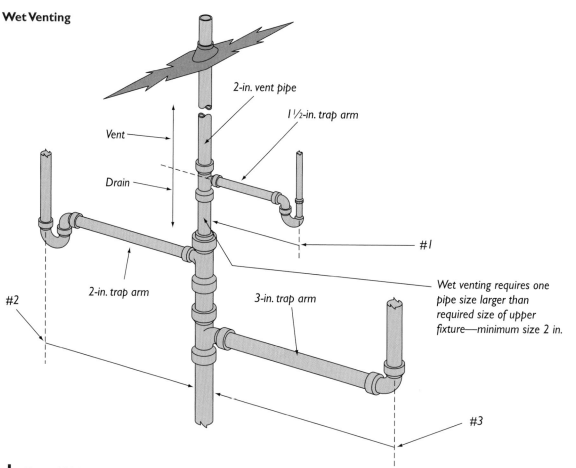

2-in. vent pipe

1½-in. trap arm

Vent

Drain

#1

2-in. trap arm

#2

3-in. trap arm

Wet venting requires one pipe size larger than required size of upper fixture—minimum size 2 in.

#3

1. For a 1½-in. trap arm, typically used for washbasins, bathtubs, and whirlpool-type tubs, the maximum run is 42 in. to the vent pipe. Once you exceed the maximum run, the drain needs to be 2 in. between the vent pipe and the soil pipe.

2. For a 2-in. trap arm, typically used for showers, dual washbasins, and laundry facilities, the maximum run is 60 in.

3. For a 3-in. trap arm, used for toilets, the maximum run is 72 in.

Dry venting systems

In your area, you might be required to install a dry venting system. This means that each fixture, except the toilet, needs a 1½-in. vent pipe that runs vertically and then horizontally (with a ¼-in. to 1-ft. slope upward) to connect back into a 3-in. main vent. The minimum-size vent pipe for a

toilet is 2 in. Plumbing codes allow changing the direction of the vent pipe from vertical to horizontal at a point lower than 6 in. above the highest fixture it serves, provided drainage fittings are used.

The bottom drawing on the facing page shows the horizontal vent 42 in. off the finish floor. The 42 in. maximum height for the trap arm distance is a plumber's "rule of thumb." This rule came about because the kitchen sink, set at 36 in., is the plumb-

✔ According to Code

The code requires pipe supports every 4 ft. for horizontal plastic pipes, as well as support for unusual configurations. Try economical plastic pipe-hanging straps and use roofing nails, which have larger heads and are less likely to slip through the strap holes.

1 ½-in. to 2-in. Drainpipe Requirements

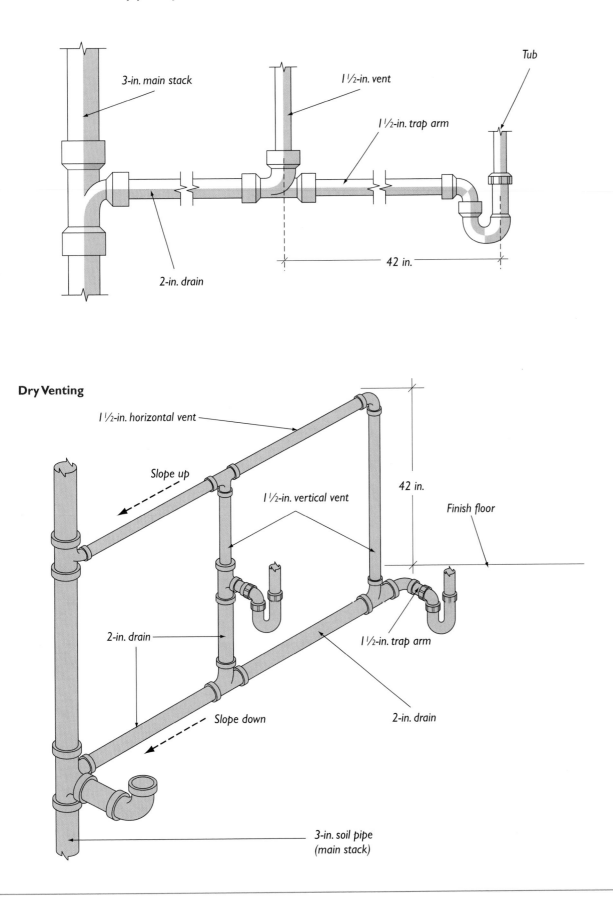

3-in. main stack

1 ½-in. vent

Tub

1 ½-in. trap arm

2-in. drain

42 in.

Dry Venting

1 ½-in. horizontal vent

Slope up

1 ½-in. vertical vent

42 in.

Finish floor

2-in. drain

1 ½-in. trap arm

2-in. drain

Slope down

3-in. soil pipe
(main stack)

PRO TIP

If you don't have a dielectric fitting to connect copper to galvanized pipe, use a brass adapter as called for in the plumbing code.

IN DETAIL

Should you plumb using ¾-in. or ½-in. copper lines? If you anticipate future expansion, I recommend ¾ in. You can do both hot and cold water lines at the hot water tank, plumbing them to the main source, and then use ½ in. lines to individual fixtures.

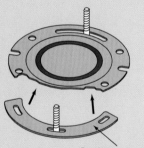

Replacement part

WHAT CAN GO WRONG

It's not unusual to discover that a section of the flange where the bolts hold the toilet in place is broken. This could be costly to replace. A simple fix is a replacement part (Fix-A-Flange by Fernco®), which fits all cast-iron, plastic, copper, and brass toilet flanges. Remove the wax toilet bowl gasket and clean the area. Then position the replacement part in the broken portion of the toilet flange. Install a new gasket and reconnect the toilet.

Redirecting Vent Pipe Less Than 6 in. Above the Flood Rim

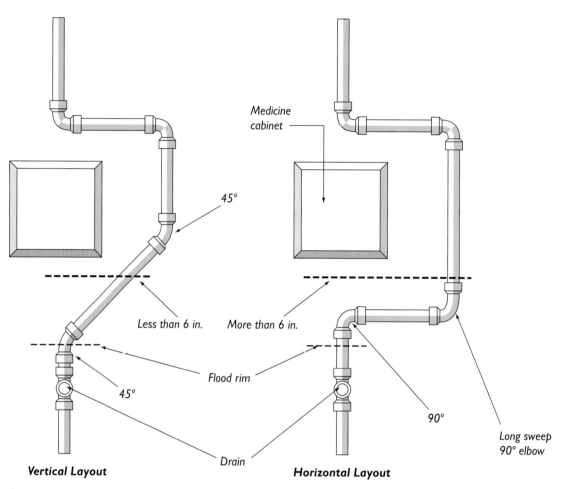

Medicine cabinet

45°

Less than 6 in.   More than 6 in.

Flood rim

45°

90°

Long sweep 90° elbow

Drain

Vertical Layout   **Horizontal Layout**

ing fixture in the house set highest off the floor. Because the code requires a vent to be 6 in. above a fixture's flood rim (the level where the fixture will begin to overflow), the vent for a kitchen sink needs to be placed at 36 in. plus 6 in., or 42 in. from the floor. This measurement simplifies vent layout for plumbers because it serves as a safe zone for all vent installations, in both kitchens and bathrooms. The maximum measurements for the trap arm distance on a wet venting system apply to dry venting systems as well.

Redirecting vent pipe

As you work with your plumbing configurations to meet plumbing codes, you'll discover that a recessed medicine cabinet above a washbasin can put a real kink in your venting plans. The vent pipe is designed to go straight up, but if you discover that the medicine cabinet is in the way, a little pipe redirection will be in order. This task can be accomplished pretty easily by cutting the vent piping above and below the medicine cabinet so you can redirect it to one side or the other.

Keep in mind that you must allow enough room for framing and new vent fittings. The other factor in this configuration is the flood rim of the fixture, which will determine what fittings to use. If you are less than 6 in. above the flood rim, you need to use drainage fittings (i.e., 45° elbows), not vent fittings. (Vent fittings may not drain properly when water enters them if the fitting is less than 6 in. above the flood rim.)

In the horizontal layout drawing on the facing page, a drainage fitting rather than a vent fitting is used to meet plumbing codes. You will need to comply with the codes in force in your area. If you are more than 6 in. above the flood rim, then you can use a 90° vent elbow.

A 45° elbow is considered "vertical" while a 90° elbow is considered "horizontal." If your existing vent pipe is ABS or PVC, use the same type of material to complete the redirection. If your existing vent pipe is galvanized, cut the pipe with a metal saw, construct the rerouting pipe in ABS or PVC, and then reconnect it to the galvanized ends using no-hub shielded couplings.

Venting through the roof

Now that you've constructed a venting system for your bathroom, where does it go? Individual vents (1½ in.) generally run up through exterior or interior walls to the roof. Actually, getting your vent pipe to the roof is more difficult than getting the pipe through it. Sometimes you have to install the vent from the roof down to the bathroom. If you don't have access to the attic, you might have to create a hole. You may find yourself opening up some finished walls if your vent pipe needs to run more than a story or two.

Installing the vent pipe. Once you've gotten your vent pipe to the roof, drill a pilot hole from the attic. I find it helpful to disconnect the drill bit from my drill and leave the drill bit in the hole in order to find my hole once I'm up on the roof. After you locate the bit, carefully remove enough roofing material so you can see the work area. Cold weather may make some roofing materials brittle, so take care bending them back; warm them if necessary. Be sure to save the pieces of roofing for reinstallation.

After removing the 3-tab roofing material down to the roof deck, I am able to position the vent pipe flashing.

With the flashing in place, I can reinstall the 3-tab roofing material, trimming it around the flashing collar. Now the vent pipe needs to be cut for height.

Remove the bit and tarpaper so you can see the wood of the roof deck, and then remove any nails or staples that may interfere with your cut. Now, use a hole saw ¼ in. to ½ in. larger than your vent piping to make your cut.

Bring the pipe up through the roof and, for a roof with a maximum 6:12 pitch (6-in. rise to a 12-in. run), extend the pipe a minimum of 12 in. above the roof. Your local codes may call for a higher clearance, so consult your building department before beginning your installation.

Slide the vent flashing down over the vent pipe so the longer portion of the tapered neck slopes down the roof. Refit the roofing material so a course runs under the lower portion of the flashing; nail the flashing in place at the top with galvanized roofing nails. Reinstall the next courses, working from the bottom up and cutting them to overlap the flashing and fit around the vent-pipe collar.

TRADE SECRET

When there's water in the line, the joint will not get hot enough to take solder, so drain all water from the lines. Try plugging existing pipes with bread. It will absorb moisture and disintegrate when the water is turned on.

If the solder lumps up on the pipe when applied, the pipe and fitting are not hot enough to form a good joint. Overheating the joint will allow the solder to run through without creating a seal. If the solder melts smoothly but does not run around the pipe, you didn't use enough flux. Apply flux around the pipe and fitting, heat evenly, and try soldering again. If it doesn't take this time, take the fitting apart, clean both the fitting and end of pipe, and start the process again.

These engineered copper fittings are used with the solder-less ProPress System.

Dealing with Copper Water Supply Lines

By now you should have a good handle on drains and venting, so it's time to focus on water supply lines, either ½-in. or ¾-in. copper pipe. Rigid copper pipe comes in three grades, but type M, the thinnest and least expensive, is suitable for most household plumbing. When you purchase copper tubing at your local home center, look for the grade information stamped on the tubing. Included there will be the pipe diameter, the wall-thickness grade, and a stamp of approval from the American Society for Testing and Materials (ASTM)ᔆᴹ.

Copper tubing and fittings

Copper tubing and fittings are similar in design to ABS and PVC pipes and fittings. The main difference is that rigid copper pipes and fittings must be soldered together. As with plastic, you'll use fitting adapters to attach copper pipes to gal-vanized pipes, but be aware that the code prohibits you from using copper adapters. Instead, special dielectric fittings have been designed for this application; they have built-in insulators to stop the electro-chemical reaction between the two different types of metals. The transfer of molecules from one metal to another causes premature corrosion.

Soldering copper fittings

To construct your copper water supply system, you'll need to create solid leak-proof bonds between the pipes and fittings by soldering the pieces together. The process involves heating the pipe and fitting to a temperature high enough to melt the solder and draw it into and around the joint. Once the joint has cooled, the strength of that joint is equal to, or even greater than, the strength of the copper pipe itself.

Cutting copper tubing

For clean cuts in copper tubing, make sure you purchase top quality tubing cutters. A full-size cutter is used for cutting copper pipe up to 1½ in. A push on the release trigger allows you to pull or lower the cutter wheel on the material, whether it's copper, brass, aluminum tubing, or thin-wall conduit. The mini tubing cutter is used for cutting hard and soft copper tubing up to ¾ in. and works well to make cuts in restricted spaces. These tools are also great for plumbing repairs.

+ SAFETY FIRST

When soldering, wear gloves, a long-sleeved shirt, and eye protection to prevent burning yourself. Never stand under a joint when soldering as the hot solder may drip. Instead, work off to the side from a stepladder.

First, cut the pipe to length. Place the cutter over the tube and tighten the roller firmly to the tube—but not so tight that it compresses the tube or that you are unable to turn the cutter. Next turn the cutter around the tube. When you have made one complete revolution, tighten the roller. Keep tightening with each complete revolution until the tube is finally cut.

Preparing the surface

Once the pipe has been cut, remove the burrs from both the inside diameter (I. D.) and the outside diameter (O. D.) of the tube. You can clean the I. D. with a flat metal reamer normally included on the tube cutter and the O. D. with emery paper. To achieve good soldered joints, the mating surfaces must be absolutely and unconditionally clean so the filler metal (solder) can sweat the surfaces easily and evenly—the cleaner the surface, the easier the sweating process. Sweating is the process whereby the solder draws itself up to flow evenly in and around the joint, and then bonds to the surfaces. If the copper is dirty, the solder balls up and adheres to itself, not to the copper. These areas then cause voids in the solder joints and create leaks in the system.

Clean about ½-in. more of the tube than the depth of the fitting sockets. The inside of the fit-

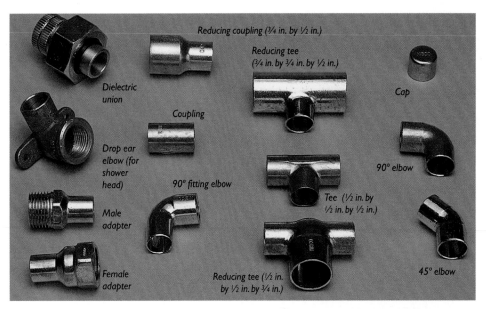

Your water supply system will be made up of these different types of copper fittings.

ting is a joint surface, and it is very important that this area also be cleaned to the same standard as the copper tubing. Even though it is shiny and new, clean the fitting socket with a special wire brush made especially for this purpose. Purchase a

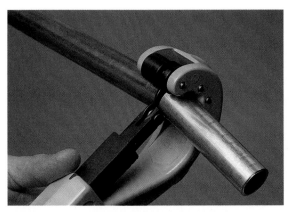

Mark with a black permanent marker where you want to cut and then cut the tube to length using a tube cutter.

Both ½-in. and ¾-in. copper can be cleaned with this four-in-one cleaning tool. The brushes mounted in the plastic handle are replaceable.

IN DETAIL

When soldering, protect flammable surfaces from the torch flame. Create a heat block with a fireproof pad or a double layer of 26-gauge sheet metal. Hold either in place with spring clamps. Also, when you're sweating shower valves, remove the working mechanism so it doesn't melt. If possible, presolder the shower valve before installing it into the framing member.

quality unit that combines cleaning brushes for both tubes and fittings into one hand tool. High-carbon steel quickly brushes clean ½-in. or ¾-in. nominal tubes and fittings in preparation for soldering. Be careful not to overclean, especially when using emery cloth; copper is a soft metal and it doesn't take much to reduce the size of the tube.

Before soldering the joints, you need one more ingredient: lead-free solder flux. Flux usually comes in a paste form—the code requires that you use "water-soluble" flux—and contains a mild acid that, when applied, covers the area to be soldered and protects it from oxidation. The mild acid is slightly corrosive and has a cleaning action.

Apply flux with a clean brush in a thin, even layer to the outside of the copper pipe and the inside of the fitting, and use only enough flux to properly cover the surfaces to be joined. Too much flux will interfere with the soldering process.

Assemble joints as soon as they are cleaned and fluxed. Align the tube and fitting so they are straight and square. They should be supported horizontally as well as vertically while you are soldering to prevent misalignment at the next joint down the piping path. Use wire or string to immobilize the joint until it has set.

Applying solder

Now you are ready for the final steps: heating the joints and applying solder. First, you need a torch that runs on propane (or a similar fuel) and lead-free solid-wire solder. You can rent a professional hand torch with a rubber hose connected to a standing gas tank or you can purchase a portable hand-held torch, an all-in-one unit with a disposable gas cylinder. Use the pencil-flame orifice to heat the fitting, and keep the flame far enough away from the fitting so that the sharp point of the inner cone of the flame just touches the metal. The larger outer envelope of the flame will then evenly spread the heat.

Heat an elbow at its back center so it heats both ends at the same time. This torch uses a brazing flame orifice for faster heating of the fitting.

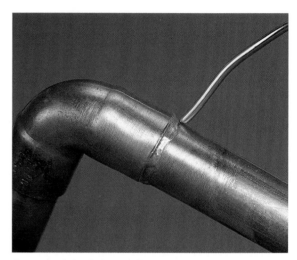

Once the joint is hot, pull the flame away from the fitting and touch the solder on the joint at one location. The flux will help draw the solder up, into, and around the joint.

While heating the area to be soldered, touch it with the solid-wire solder from time to time to see if it melts. When the solder begins to melt, even a little, move the flame to the heel or center of the fitting. Manipulate the flame so that the entire fitting is hot and at the same time feed the solder into the joint. Do not melt the solder in the flame—once the joint is hot, pull the flame away from the fitting and touch the solder on the joint at one location. There's no need to move the solder around the joint; the flux will help draw the solder up, in, and around the joint. Some plumbers will keep the flame on the fitting when applying the solder. When the joint looks full, they'll remove the flame and then apply solder around the joint again. This method can be used as long as the tube is hot enough to melt the solder.

This step is not required, but if you want to produce a clean-looking joint, use a damp cloth to wipe away any excess solder and flux. Do this at once, while the joint is still hot. Be careful—the pipe is very hot, so keep your fingers on the damp cloth and don't touch the pipe. The joint will cool very quickly in air.

A solderless system

For the copper tubing work in my bathroom, I chose a new solderless copper system called ProPress®. The system uses a series of engineered copper fittings in over 240 configurations and in sizes ranging from ½ in. to 2 in., as well as bronze adapters. A special electro-hydraulic crimping tool crimps the fitting to the pipe. The ethylene propylene diene monomer (EPDM) seal made of a high-performance elastomer is designed to last the life of the tubing. After the fitting is crimped, the copper tubing and sealing elements form a permanent watertight seal. Fittings are rated at 200 psi working pressure, 600 psi tested pressure, and a temperature range of 0°F to 250°F. However, the tool is cumbersome, and at times I found there wasn't enough room to use it.

Before you move on to electrical, your rough-in plumbing needs to be tested to ensure that all the joints are securely bonded and the system is leak-proof. Check with your local municipality for code requirements and their preferred method of testing—either air or water. The system needs to be able to hold one or the other for fifteen minutes. An inspection is also required at this time.

Clamps Required by Code

Securing pipes is required by code. For 1½-in. copper pipe, you'll need supply-pipe hangers every 6 ft. horizontally and no more than every 10 ft. vertically. Pipe hangers, or clamps—made of polyethylene or metal—absorb tubing movement and can eliminate any contact between pipes and framing surfaces. The ribbed design of these clamps permits faster cooling and allows the pipe to expand and contract with less noise. If you choose metal clamps, straps, or hangers for your copper supply lines, make sure they are also copper. Other metals are known to react chemically with copper.

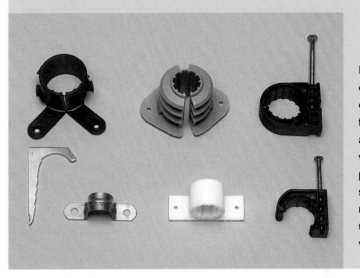

Pipe clamps come in a variety of configurations for different applications and will hold your plumbing securely while reducing the transmission of water line noise.

The ProPress System can crimp a fitting (as shown on p. 56) even with water in the pipe, something that cannot be done when sweating copper pipes. The system saves on labor time, but it does have to be installed by a professional.

Electrical

CHAPTER FOUR
Rough-In

A s with a plumbing rough-in, it's easier to plan and execute your new wiring with the walls exposed down to the studs. This open framing allows you to inspect—and possibly change—existing wiring. It also gives you access to install new rough-in electrical. In addition, you'll save time and the frustration of fishing cable through finished walls.

The electrical rough-in is about planning exactly where your fixtures will go, running the wiring, and installing boxes. Even if your studs aren't exposed, switches can be relocated, vanity lights and fans can be wired, and GFCI receptacles can be added. This is also the time to reconnect any wiring that was disconnected because it interfered with rough-in framing or plumbing.

This chapter will provide simple step-by-step instructions to help you confidently plan the electrical circuits, and safely install wiring and boxes in preparation for your electrical inspection.

PRO TIP

Place peel-and-stick numbers where you plan to locate fixtures. Wait a short time and check again to see if you still like the layout.

IN DETAIL

Mirrors pose challenges when it comes to lighting. Lights along the sides will more evenly light your face, but you may prefer the look of lights above the mirror. It comes down to personal preference, type of mirror, ceiling height, available wall space on both sides of the mirror, and how you plan to use the mirror.

Our ceiling is higher than 8 ft., so it allows room for crown molding. Because of the crown molding, a light above the mirror was not appropriate. We decided on sidelights that complemented the style of the mirror. To improve the mirror's function, we installed a ceiling flush-mount light controlled by a dimmer switch. The "egg-and-dart" mirror frame matches the crown molding, which, with the rope-tile backsplash and side-lights, pulls the theme together.

This flush-mount light looks expensive but really isn't. It provides a touch of class to the finished project.

Locating Fixtures

My wife and I discovered that as the bathroom came together, we were beginning to visualize design possibilities that were different from our original plan. Again we selected lights, an exhaust fan, and a heat lamp, and determined their placement in the bathroom.

You, too, may face these challenges at this phase of the project. Don't hesitate to rethink your plan—now is the time to make any adjustments.

Lighting options

A well-thought-out lighting design can transform an average bath into one that's both functional and soothing. Start by organizing your design plan into three categories: task lighting, ambient lighting, and accent lighting.

Task lighting. Many individuals mount a light fixture over the vanity or medicine cabinet without realizing that it will cast a shadow over their faces. If possible, place lights alongside your mirror. Over the tub/shower area, use an Underwriters' Laboratories (UL)-rated recessed

Basic Wiring Projects

Here are a few wiring projects you're likely to encounter as you rough-in the electrical for your bathroom remodel:

- Receptacles: Installing GFCI and other receptacles.
- Lighting: Installing an overhead light, night-light, and vanity lighting.
- Ventilation: Installing a vented fan.
- Heating: Installing a wall, floor, ceiling, or toekick heater, radiant heat (floor-warming system), and heat lamps.

✓ According to Code

To install a recessed uninsulated fixture (light, heat lamp, etc.) that emits heat in an area near insulation or framing, you'll need to construct a code-compliant barrier around the unit. It's safer and easier to install a unit labeled "IC" (Insulation Contact).

fixture with a waterproof gasket to protect against heavy moisture. Alternatively, install a heat lamp close to the shower area and consider using a red, mood-enhancing, infrared bulb.

Ambient lighting. Ambient lighting, which acts as a substitute for natural light, is generally provided by the overhead ceiling fixture. As well as defining the bathroom space, it provides a soft overall illumination and allows safe movement in the room. The atmosphere of the room—warm or cool—depends on the colors and textures used and how the ambient lighting plays off them. For a softer approach, consider putting a dimmer switch on the overhead light.

Indirect lighting, a form of ambient lighting, uses one or more luminaries (fixtures) to throw light onto the ceiling and upper walls of a room. This is also called uplighting. Indirect lighting minimizes shadows and reflected glare that bounces off the ceiling. Uplighting is particularly useful when using glossy paper or reflective surfaces such as computer or television screens.

Accent lighting. For a dramatic feel, consider including small recessed spotlights in your plans. Directed at a decorative object or a stylish countertop, this type of lighting creates a more sophisticated look.

Exhaust fans

More than any room in the house, a bath needs proper ventilation because it's constantly exposed to water, moisture, and bathroom odors. While the walls and ceiling are open, take the opportunity to address this issue. Follow the manufacturer's recommendations for locating the fan in your bathroom. Usually, the fan will go into the ceiling at the dead center of the tub/shower's length and roughly a foot outside the tub/shower area. Make-up air (air needed to replace air being exhausted by the fan) is required for proper ventilation. It can be provided by a ½-in. gap (minimum) between the bottom of

A simple but elegant ceramic night-light adds gentle ambient light.

When installing fixtures that have adjustable hanging extension bars, securely fasten the ends of the bars to the framing material with staples, nails, or screws. A trial run can help determine how much to cut off each extension bar. Notice that the joists were cut and a pocket was created to allow the fan and ductwork to be installed.

PRO TIP

Purchasing a few extra electrical parts may help avoid time-wasting trips to the local home center for replacements.

IN DETAIL

Besides purchasing a fan with enough cfms to handle the room's moisture load, check the sone ratings on the packaging: the lower the number, the quieter the fan. The goal is to find a fan with a low sone number and a high cfm rating. Sones offer an easy way to compare loudness—double the sone is double the loudness.

WHAT CAN GO WRONG

Plan switch box placement carefully. If you use a 3½-in.-wide casing, there won't be adequate space for a switch plate on the double studs of the door opening. A spacer will be needed to pull the switch box away from the edge of the casing. Check your measurement before the switch box is nailed.

Choosing the Proper Fan

The more cfms the fan has, the more powerful the unit is. To select a fan with adequate venting power or cfm rating, use one of the following calculation methods recommended by the fan industry:

- For an 8-ft. ceiling, multiply the square footage of the room by 1.1. For example, for a 5-ft. by 9-ft. bathroom, multiply 45 sq. ft. by 1.1, which equals 49.5.
- Alternatively, for any ceiling height, multiply the cu. ft. of the room (W x L x H) by 8 (recommended air changes per hour) and divide it by 60 (the number of minutes in an hour). For example, a 5-ft. by 9-ft. by 8-ft. bathroom has 360 cubic feet. Multiply that by 8 and divide it by 60 to get 48.

In both cases, a 50-cfm fan would meet the minimum requirements, but I would consider purchasing a 90-cfm (or higher) fan to adequately handle the moisture.

Warmth Beneath Your Feet

In our bathroom, we chose an electric floor-warming system. We ruled out an electric heater in the wall because we were striving for more open wall surface. SunTouch's floor mat kit includes all the parts necessary to complete the system—a wall-mounted thermostat, a floor temperature sensor, and double-sided tape to secure the mat. The system can be installed over a wooden subfloor or concrete slab and adds ⅛ in. to the floor height. It is important, however, to insulate under the concrete slab to direct the heat into the room.

To begin, secure the orange mat with double-sided tape and staples. A thinset mortar tops the mat, and then the finish floor can be installed. Work carefully when applying the mortar to prevent damage to the heating elements. Use the flat side of the trowel and apply a first coat of thinset, just enough to cover the elements. I used a premix thinset, but I wouldn't recommend it—it's too thick to spread and doesn't allow thinning. Instead, purchase a modified thinset that has all the required additives (such as VersaBond® bonding mortar by Custom Building Products®) that will

Thinset mortar tops the mat and then the finish floor can be installed.

allow you to thin the product for smooth, easy troweling. I also recommend "LoudMouth," a device by SunTouch that connects to the mat during the installation. It monitors the heating elements, and, if the elements are severed or come in contact with the ground shield, the device will sound an alarm. Also test the unit before applying thinset by temporarily laying loose tile over the mat and heating elements, installing the thermostat, and turning it on. Once you are satisfied, turn off the breaker, remove the thermostat, hook up "LoudMouth," and apply the thinset mortar.

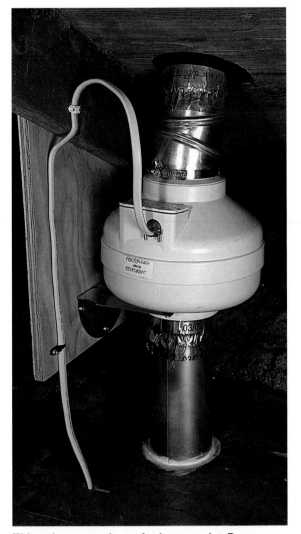

This attic-mounted vent fan is very quiet. Because the hole in the roof is slightly off target, I used an adjustable elbow to connect to the roof vent cap. Where the pipe passes through the attic deck has been sealed with latex caulk.

Heat

The third major consideration for any bathroom is heating. If your existing system doesn't provide enough warmth, you might want to add a wall-mounted electric heater, a unit in the toekick of the vanity, heat lamps, or a ceiling combination unit (heater/fan/light). If, like me, you enjoy padding around the house in bare feet, think about installing radiant heat or a floor-warming system in the bathroom floor.

Consider what I call the "treat me" fixtures or the "wish I'd known about it before I finished" products. These include a wall-mounted hairdryer located near the vanity, a built-in iron-ing center for the bath/laundry room, or an electric towel warmer for those who enjoy warm towels.

the door and the finish floor. Larger cfm fans will require more make-up air, which can be provided through a larger gap under the door or by installing a forced-air diffuser.

Also available are combination heat lamps with exhaust fans. The Deflect-o tube–style fan vents bathroom moisture to the outside through the roof.

Perhaps a ventilating fan/light combination unit is on your wish list. Some turn on automatically, triggered by motion, humidity, or both.

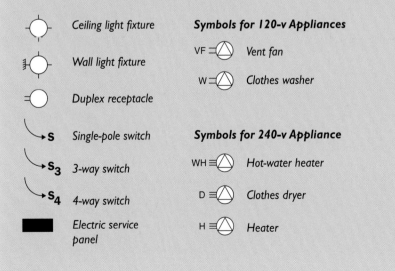

Electrical Symbols

If you have ever seen a set of architectural plans, you might have noticed (but not understood) the electrical symbols. Here are some of the standard symbols and their meanings. A solid line shows wires in ceilings or walls; a dotted line shows wires in or under the floor. When drawing your bathroom plans, use these standard symbols to help lay out your electrical work; that way you won't forget anything during the later stages of remodeling.

Ceiling light fixture

Wall light fixture

Duplex receptacle

S Single-pole switch

S₃ 3-way switch

S₄ 4-way switch

Electric service panel

Symbols for 120-v Appliances

VF Vent fan

W Clothes washer

Symbols for 240-v Appliance

WH Hot-water heater

D Clothes dryer

H Heater

PRO TIP

PRO TIP

Before using any tester on electrical wiring, check it out on a circuit that you know is live.

A voltage tester is used to check this 30-amp double-pole breaker to an electric hot water tank to make sure it's not live. With breakers in the off position, the red probe is placed on the breaker's screw terminal and the black probe on the neutral bar. Each breaker needs to be tested this way. Take care when working in a live service panel box.

WHAT CAN GO WRONG

Electricity must always complete a circuit to function correctly. If the current's circular path is interrupted, electricity will not flow throughout the system, causing receptacles to fail. If, for example, a hot wire should come loose and touch a grounded metal receptacle box, the grounding wire will divert the current and channel it safely to the neutral bar. If the box were not grounded, it would be electrically live. If you touched that ungrounded box, your body would provide the electrical path through which the current could flow—and you'd receive a severe shock.

Learning Wiring Basics

Now that you have an idea about where you'd like your fixtures to go, you'll need to map out how to bring in the wiring to power them safely. A typical bathroom requires at least one 20-amp circuit for the receptacles and one 15-amp circuit to power the lights and fan. Additional circuits may be required if your plans call for radiant heat, a wall heater, or a whirlpool-type tub.

Examining your current wiring

Take time to study preexisting wiring in exposed walls and/or ceiling framing members for insights on how electrical wires run from the panel box to the receptacles, switches, and all the fixtures—the lights, the heater, and the fan.

If, after you read this chapter, you feel uncomfortable with this phase of the project, hire an electrician and watch the work being done— you'll be ready to tackle the wiring on your next

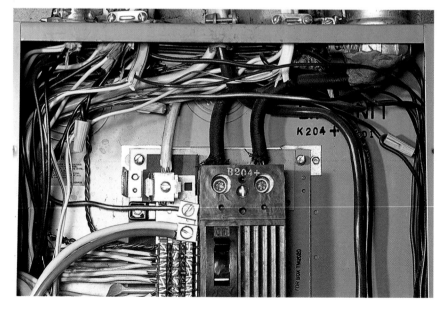

The white (neutral) wire (left) is connected to the neutral bus bar where both white neutral and grounding wires are connected. Just to the right of the white neutral wire are the two black hot wires (center and right) that feed into the main disconnect.

All about GFCI Receptacles

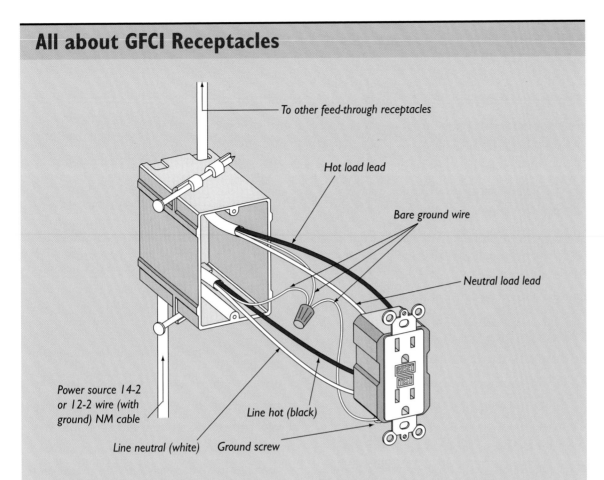

To other feed-through receptacles

Hot load lead

Bare ground wire

Neutral load lead

Power source 14-2 or 12-2 wire (with ground) NM cable

Line hot (black)

Line neutral (white)   Ground screw

GFCIs are required by code in new and remodeled bathrooms, whirlpool-type tubs, and indoor hot tubs. This receptacle is a safety device that monitors the equal flow of electricity through the hot (black) wire and the neutral (white) wire. It shuts itself off automatically (in about $25/1000$ of a second) if a current leakage to ground exceeds 5 milliamps (1 milliamp equals $1/1000$ of an amp) in the circuit. This reduces the danger of current leakage and the possibility of shock hazard if you touch an improperly grounded appliance or light fixture.

A bathroom remodeling project could call for either a GFCI receptacle or a GFCI breaker. The breaker fits into the service panel just like a standard breaker, except the neutral wire from the circuit cable connects to the neutral lug of the GFCI breaker, and the neutral pigtail on the GFCI breaker connects to the neutral

bar in the panel. Be careful not to confuse the white pigtail with the white wire in the cable. This type of breaker is great for a single circuit to a whirlpool-type tub.

As required by the National Electrical Code (NEC), all receptacles in a bathroom are required to be GFCI-protected, and nothing else can be on the circuit except those bathroom receptacles. Receptacles located within 3 ft. of any washbasin, even in a laundry room, for example, must also be GFCI-protected. It is also important to know that a GFCI breaker must have its own individual circuit.

A GFCI receptacle is designed with built-in ground-fault protection that can be installed to provide GFCI protection through itself alone, or it can be wired to feed through other standard receptacles protecting all or part of a branch circuit.

PRO TIP

Buy the same brand of receptacles and switches; check to see if they are all screw terminals or combination screw terminals and push-in outlets.

IN DETAIL

A circuit breaker exposed to excessive heat will trip to the "off" position or to an intermediate position. Sometimes when the breaker has not quite made it to that intermediate position—or if the breaker doesn't have a little window through which you can see—it's hard to determine if it has tripped or not. If the manufacturer of your service panel permits their use, purchase circuit breakers with those little windows; they will make it easier to see if the breaker really has tripped. In any case, when breakers trip, they can be reset. Depending on the breaker, you have to force the handle beyond the "off" position and then click it back on, or you can just move it to the "on" position.

project. If you decide to carry on, make sure that you never work with the power on.

Testing the electrical current

Once you've turned off the power, use a neon circuit tester or voltage tester to confirm that the line is dead. The neon circuit tester is less expensive, but I prefer the voltage tester because it helps me to identify whether I'm on a 120-v or 240-v line. Since it makes a sound to indicate a hot circuit, I don't have to be looking at it to know. Once you've tripped the circuit breaker, check the line at the junction boxes, receptacles, switches, and fixtures.

Making sure your service is adequate

Thirty years ago, most homes had 100-amp to 125-amp service. In newer homes, though, a minimum of 200-amp service is generally considered necessary for today's electrical needs. The number of circuits required for your bathroom is dictated by the fixtures you wish to install, the require-

ments of the fixture manufacturers, and the electrical code in your area.

Typically:

- Lights need a minimum 15-amp circuit and outlets need a 20-amp circuit. Bathroom outlets must be on their own circuit and must be GFCI-protected.
- A fan is wired into the lighting circuitry.
- A whirlpool-type tub requires a 20-amp circuit.
- A whirlpool-type tub heater needs a 20-amp circuit, depending on the heater's size.
- A room heater may require a 20-amp circuit.
- A heat lamp requires a separate 20-amp circuit, depending on the manufacturer's requirements.

If your service is not adequate, consider hiring an electrician to solve the problem. Besides checking the service box, an electrician will verify that the system is properly grounded to two grounding rods (driven 8 ft. into the ground and 6 ft. apart) and a metal cold water pipe.

In the panel box, the wires are connected to individual breakers, creating 120-v and 240-v circuits. These circuits use individual breakers (single- or double-pole) within the panel box.

This grounding clamp secures the grounding wire from the panel box to a galvanized cold water line. The system is not complete until a grounding wire leaves the neutral bar and is attached to two 8-ft. grounding rods spaced 6 ft. apart.

The 15-amp slim breaker (left) uses 14-gauge wire and the 20-amp breaker (right) uses 12-gauge wire. Two slims could take the place of one normal-sized breaker, such as the 20-amp breaker shown.

They are independent switches—once on, they deliver power to the branch circuits and then, for example, to a receptacle, appliance, or fixture.

Circuit breakers

Circuit breakers protect the electrical circuit from damage caused by too much current. If forced to carry more electricity than the wiring can safely handle, they'll trip, breaking the circuit and turning off the power. A faulty receptacle, switch, appliance, or a power overload caused by having too many appliances on one circuit can all contribute to a breaker tripping. Power surges from the utility company or lightning can also cause breakers to trip.

Circuit breakers must be rated for the same current as the wiring they protect. A 14-gauge wire can safely handle 15 amps. If a 20-amp breaker is used with 14-gauge wire, the 20-amp breaker will not trip should the circuit overload. Instead, the wire becomes the breaker and will heat up, perhaps enough to cause a fire. A 15-amp breaker should be used with 14-gauge wire. A 20-amp breaker is designed to be used with 12-gauge wire.

Drawing a wiring diagram

Wiring diagrams are essential to your electrical rough-in. They help you to organize your plan by walking you through the project on paper, and they are key to creating a materials list.

Most bathroom remodels involve a few essential wiring projects. The most common is installing an overhead light and the single-pole switch to turn it on and off. This project is a building block for other, more complicated, wiring installations, and is described later in this chapter.

Calculating electrical needs

Proper watt calculations can prevent blown fuses or tripped breakers. To correctly wire your bathroom, it's essential to understand the energy

---

Wiring Circuit Breakers

A 120-v circuit is one breaker. The hot wire (normally black) is attached to the breaker, the white wire is attached to the neutral bar, and the ground wire (bare) is connected to the ground bar. (This neutral bar, when grounded to the panel, serves as both a neutral and a ground bar.) For a 240-v circuit, a double breaker (two 120-v circuits) is required. One black wire (hot) will connect to one breaker, and a white wire (hot) will connect to the other breaker. The ground wire is connected to the ground and/or neutral bar in the panel box.

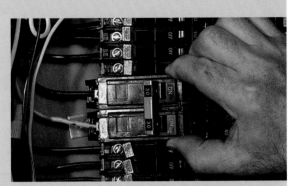

Use a double-pole breaker with 240-v circuits.

---

requirements of your appliances and fixtures in relation to the amount of wattage your electrical circuit can carry. The actual flow of electricity is determined by the energy requirements (watts) of the fixtures and appliances in use at a given time.

For example, a typical bathroom might require:

- An exhaust fan at **30** watts.
- A two-bulb (**60** watts each) ceiling light at **120** watts.
- One heat lamp at **250** watts or a two-lamp fixture at **500**.
- Two sidelights (**60** watts each) at **120** watts.
- A cordless electric toothbrush charger at **1.5** watts.
- A hairdryer at **1500** watts or more.

A **14-gauge wire** (15-amp breaker), used for the exhaust fan, lights, and heat lamp, can handle up to 1800 watts before it becomes overloaded.

A **12-gauge wire** (20-amp breaker), used for receptacles for a hairdryer, curling iron, or electric toothbrush, can handle up to 2400 watts.

PRO TIP

Be sure to position boxes with captive nails at the proper depth—if the box misses its mark, the nails are hard to remove.

IN DETAIL

A pigtail extends wire length, making multiple or stiff single wires, e.g., 12-gauge, more manageable. A 12-gauge wire with a 14-gauge pigtail is much easier to connect to a switch or outlet and push into a box. Use the same color pigtail wire as the wires to be connected using wire nuts. Here, grounding wires are tied together with a crimp connector. One wire was cut off; the other (pigtail) is being connected to the ground screw. Pigtailing the black and white wires would have left only two wires in the back of the outlet.

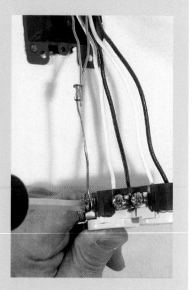

Common Bathroom Circuits

Most baths will have at least two main circuits: one for lighting and one for receptacles. A common lighting circuit begins with a 2-wire with ground 14-gauge non-metallic (NM) cable that runs from the main service panel either to a light fixture back down to a switch-box or from a switchbox to a light fixture. From there, it could feed other fixtures. The second circuit will use a 2-wire with ground 12-gauge NM cable to feed a GFCI receptacle that could go on to feed and provide shock protection to other standard receptacles. A vent fan with heater, a whirlpool-type tub, and electric heater, and any other major appliances will each require its own dedicated electrical circuit.

Single-Pole Switch

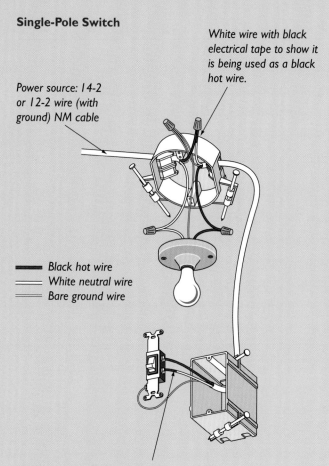

Power source: 14-2 or 12-2 wire (with ground) NM cable

White wire with black electrical tape to show it is being used as a black hot wire.

■■■ Black hot wire
——— White neutral wire
≡≡≡ Bare ground wire

White wire with black electrical tape to show it is being used as a black hot wire.

Wire Size and Capacity

Wires that are 14-gauge (for lighting and switches) and 12-gauge (for receptacles) are used in standard 120-v circuits. Wires that are 10-gauge and 8-gauge are used in 240-v circuits for large appliances, such as heaters, electric dryers, and water heaters. It is not enough just to know the gauge—you also need to know the amps (amperes) and watts that correspond to each gauge. Use this chart as a guide for how many amps and watts the various wires can handle.

Corresponding Wire Size to Amps and Watts

Wire size	Amps	Watts
14	15	1800
12	20	2400
10	30	3600
8	40	4800

An exhaust fan (**30** watts) + a light fixture (**250** watts) + overhead lights (**120** watts) + side-lights (**120** watts) = **520** watts, which can easily be handled on a 15-amp breaker, 14-gauge wire.

A cordless toothbrush (**1.5** watts) + a hairdryer (**1500** watts) = **1501.5** watts, which can easily be handled on a 20-amp breaker, 12-gauge wire.

To verify that the amp breaker can handle the wattage requirements, divide the total watts by **120** to determine amps. In the example above (hairdryer and cordless toothbrush), **1501.5** watts ÷ **120** volts = **012.51** amps, easily carried by a 20-amp breaker.

Remember to check the manufacturer's instructions for wattage requirements. A two-lamp heating fixture, floor warming system, and whirlpool-type tub will each require its own circuit.

Installing Boxes and Wiring

Electrical boxes, connector and wire nuts, receptacles, and switches are some of the electrical parts you will be using in your wiring project.

Electrical boxes

It's possible that your bathroom has metal electrical boxes. Even though it's fine to keep them, you might consider replacing them all with user-friendly plastic boxes or using plastic for just the new wiring. If the walls are open, I suggest replacing all metal boxes with plastic, providing they're not attached to conduit.

Metal boxes. There are five basic boxes on the market. The square is usually used as a junction box, but it can also be used for single or double receptacles. The octagon is used for overhead or sidewall lighting. The switch nail-on and handy with side bracket easily attach to vertical studs to serve as switches and receptacles. The handy box is designed to be mounted on a wall's surface, e.g., on a concrete wall.

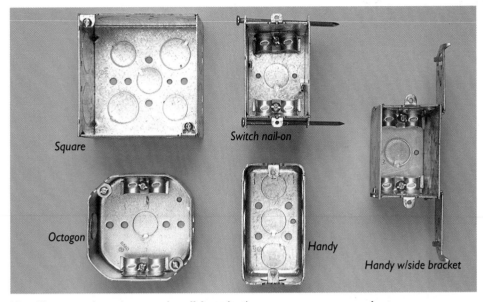

Square *Switch nail-on* *Octogon* *Handy* *Handy w/side bracket*

Metal boxes such as these work well, but plastic ones are more convenient.

Wire Specifications

Wire is manufactured in coded colors. Remember that the white wire is always neutral unless the power source flows through the light fixture to the switch. Whenever you use a wire in this type of situation, it is required by code that you place a piece of black tape around the ends of the white wire to identify it as a hot wire.

Red and black wires are used for hot wires. Green, green and yellow, and bare copper are ground wires. Two or more insulated color-coded wires combined in a non-metallic (plastic) sheath create different types of cables. (The most common of these cables used in residential electrical installations is known as Romex®.) Cables are stamped with numbers and letters, such as *Type NMB 12-2G* or *Type NMB 12-3G*. Some common classifications are explained as follows:

- Type NM means nonmetallic.
- B refers to insulation up to 90°C.
- 12 means it is a 12-gauge wire.
- 2 means two insulated wires (black and white).
- 3 means three insulated wires (black, red, and white).
- G means it has a ground wire.

Always connect the black wire to a brass or copper-colored terminal on switches and receptacles, and to the black wire of lights and fixtures. Connect the white wire to the light or silver-colored terminal of all receptacles, and to the white wire of lights and fixtures. One way to remember: light for white; brass for black.

IN DETAIL

In remodels and new construction, the NEC requires three-hole grounding receptacles. If the plan is to replace an existing ungrounded two-hole receptacle with the new style, be aware that your electrical system itself might not be grounded, so new three-hole receptacles won't accomplish anything. To wire three-hole receptacles in an ungrounded system, a ground wire must be attached to a cold water line, or you may have to run it back to the service panel. If the receptacle box is metal, ground the receptacle to the box and make sure the metal box is grounded back to the electrical panel.

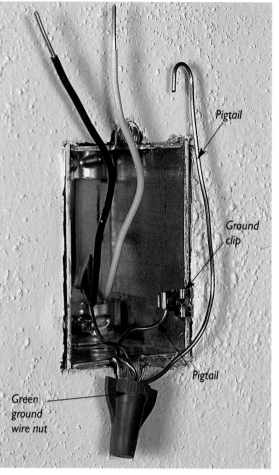

Pigtail

Ground clip

Pigtail

Green ground wire nut

Even with the ground wire attached to the box with a ground clip, the pigtail shown still needs to be attached to the ground screw on a receptacle or switch.

To fasten a vertical box to a stud, use the switch box with captive nails. Be certain of your placement; it's a hard box to move after it's nailed. The handy box with side brackets is the most user-friendly box for attaching to a stud.

Whenever you use a metal box, use wire connectors to bring wires into the box. Remove one of the knockouts, then install the wire connector so it's on the outside and the locknut is on the inside. Once secured, you can feed the wire through the connector and tighten the clamp screws. Use a plastic clamp connector that quickly snaps into place instead of traditional threaded metal clamps.

Some metal boxes conveniently have built-in clamps. Make sure that all your ground wires are tied together and grounded to the box using either a ground clip or a ground screw.

Plastic boxes. Plastic boxes are my favorite to work with because they have a depth gauge on the side of the box for easy placement, and built-in nails, as well as wire clamps located in the box at the back, for securing the cable.

Even if your bath contains metal boxes, you can still install plastic nail-on boxes. Again, be sure that

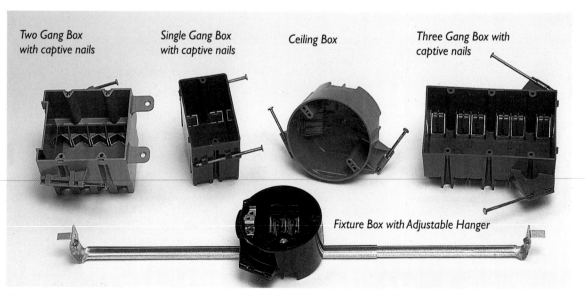

Two Gang Box with captive nails

Single Gang Box with captive nails

Ceiling Box

Three Gang Box with captive nails

Fixture Box with Adjustable Hanger

Many electrical boxes are available. Some round ceiling boxes come attached to adjustable extension brackets. Others have nailing flanges.

all ground wires are tied together between the metal and plastic boxes.

If your plan calls for a new receptacle or switch in an existing wall, but opening the wall is of some concern, consider using cut-in boxes, also known as "remodeling" or "retrofit" boxes. There are two different styles—metal saddle and flip-up tabs—and they both work well. I prefer the flip-up tabs, especially with the single- and double-gang boxes.

Receptacles

When selecting a receptacle, keep in mind that there are three basic types: side-wired, back-wired, and combination (duplex). I prefer the combination because both screw or push-in outlets (or a combination of both) can be used for continuous wiring.

When wiring, the hot (black) wire goes to the brass-colored screw and the neutral (white) wire goes to the silver-colored screw. The green screw at the bottom is for the ground wire.

The back-wired or push-in receptacles have holes in which to insert the wires. The back of the receptacle also features a strip gauge that shows how much insulation to strip off the end of the wire. Also look for the word "white" printed on the backside—that's the side for the white neutral wires. Looking at the front of the receptacle, notice the vertical plug holes—they indicate that this is a 15-amp receptacle. If the left-hand hole has a horizontal T, then it is a 20-amp receptacle.

Switches

When it's time to purchase switches, do some homework, because there are many different types and styles on the market. A basic single-pole switch controls lights from one location, a three-way switch controls lights from two locations, and a four-way switch combined with three-way switches can control a light from three or more locations. You can tell these switches apart by the number of terminal screws they have.

Single-pole switch. The single-pole switch is the most commonly used switch in the home. If you have older switches, which make a loud clicking sound when the toggle is operated, consider replacing them with quieter models. Remember that there will be times when the switch will be wired with two black (hot) wires or one black and one white wire. In this case it is important to tape both ends of the white wire with black electrical tape to indicate that this wire is indeed a live wire and is acting as a black wire.

The wiring diagrams on pp. 74 and 75 for switches and fixtures show how to connect the wiring using a single-pole or two three-way switches. The light fixtures in the diagrams are for the purpose of illustration—the diagrams could work as well for fans or heat lamps. Remember to turn the electricity off before you begin any work, take your time, and follow the codes in your area.

The drawing on p. 74 shows the power entering the switch box. The hot (black) lead is connected

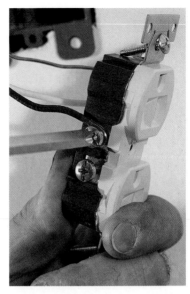

Loop the wire clockwise around the terminal screw so that the wire locks tightly against the terminal for a secure installation.

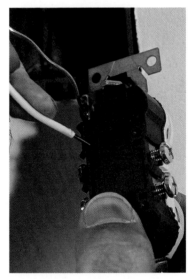

Wire, which is pushed into the wire well with these push-in outlets, is automatically clamped by spring action to ensure good electrical connection.

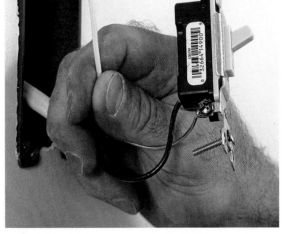

White wire has been stripped to its proper length (½ in.), and the black tape is installed just before the stripped wire to indicate it is a live wire.

PRO TIP

If the wire you plan to strip feels too loose or tight in the wire stripper, you are probably not in the proper gauge opening.

IN DETAIL

Make sure the ground wire is attached to both the switch and the light fixture. If your switch and fixture do not have ground terminals, purchase ones that do. If you're working with metal boxes, fasten ground wires to the boxes. In plastic boxes, tie all the ground wires together. Be sure to check the local codes concerning ground wires for switches and fixtures used in plastic boxes.

TRADE SECRET

Test the electrical system before installing any wallboard. Hook up the entire system and install temporary pigtail lamp holders wherever there are light-fixture boxes. This is a good way to test switches. For receptacles, purchase a receptacle circuit tester. They are inexpensive and simple to use, and they're great for fault identification in 3-wire, 120-v circuits when testing for various wiring conditions—open ground, reverse polarity, open hot, open neutral, hot and ground reversed, hot on neutral, and hot open.

Special Switches and Dimmers

These switches and dimmers offer features for easy usage and energy efficiency:

- Illuminated rocker switch. The rocker panel switch glows softly when the switch is off, providing a built-in night-light.
- Pilot light rocker switch. This model lights up when it is on.
- Passive infrared occupancy sensor switch. For incandescent or fluorescent lights, this energy-saving switch turns on when you enter a room.
- Toggle with a slide dimmer. An alternative to the popular rotary dimmer, this dimmer provides full-range lighting control with an on/off switch and a separate lever that slides up and down to regulate brightness.

Rotary (left), and toggle (right).

Single-Pole Switch

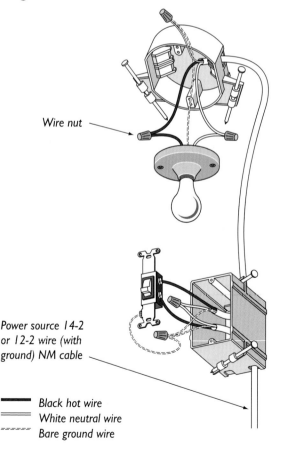

Wire nut

Power source 14-2 or 12-2 wire (with ground) NM cable

— Black hot wire
═ White neutral wire
┄ Bare ground wire

to the bottom terminal, and the neutral (white) lead is connected to the white wire going to the light. The black wire from the light is then connected to the upper terminal of the switch.

A three-way switch is used in pairs to control a light or receptacle from two separate locations. It's great for bathrooms with two doors. The switch has three terminals (screws): one black, or copper-colored, and two brass, or silver-colored. There are no "on" and "off" markings on the toggle.

Three-way switches and fixture. The drawing on the facing page shows a three-way switch with power going into the switch box and the light fixture between the two three-way switches.

Wiring cables

It's time to begin wiring your project. If the walls are completely exposed, or if there's a need to add an outlet to an existing wall, you can accomplish your wiring goals by following these directions.

Installing a remodeling outlet box

Adding an outlet box in an existing wall may appear to be a simple task—and in some cases it is—but it can also mean you'll spend a few hours fishing wires to the box. One tool you'll need for this task is an electrical fish tape, a semi-rigid wire used to pull cable.

If the ceiling below your bathroom is open, begin by drilling a 1-in. (minimum) hole up through the underside of the subfloor and bottom plate of the wall, and into the cavity of the same stud space as the existing receptacle or the cut-in box you want to wire. If the ceiling below the bathroom is covered, you'll need to expose a portion of the ceiling or work from the bathroom itself, behind a base molding, for example. Push the fish tape up through the hole drilled below until a second pair of hands can grab the tape through the existing receptacle box opening (or through a new hole cut for a cut-in box).

Always consider the length of cable you'll need. For short runs attach the new wire to the fish tape and pull it down through the receptacle opening. For long runs, attach a second fish tape to the first, pull it down through the opening until it can be reached, attach a new wire to the second tape, and then pull it back up through the opening.

+ SAFETY FIRST

Before performing any electrical work, always disconnect the electricity before you begin, either by removing the fuse or by tripping the breaker in the main panel. To make sure the power is off, use a tester to check the line you are about to work on. For a safe installation, check with your local municipality to make sure that your wiring complies with national, state or local codes.

Three-Way Switches and Fixture

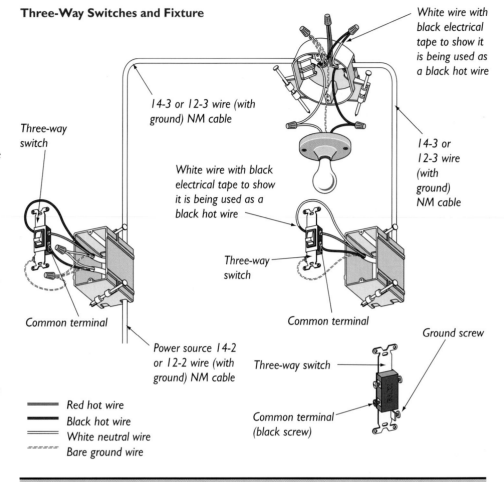

White wire with black electrical tape to show it is being used as a black hot wire

14-3 or 12-3 wire (with ground) NM cable

Three-way switch

14-3 or 12-3 wire (with ground) NM cable

White wire with black electrical tape to show it is being used as a black hot wire

Three-way switch

Common terminal

Common terminal

Ground screw

Power source 14-2 or 12-2 wire (with ground) NM cable

Three-way switch

Common terminal (black screw)

Red hot wire
Black hot wire
White neutral wire
Bare ground wire

Tips to Remember

- Set receptacle boxes so they are convenient for you. Place switch boxes 48 in. off the floor to the center of the box and remember to locate them on the same side of the doorframe as the doorknob.
- Whenever wires enter or leave a box, take time to secure the wire within 12 in. of the box with staples. It is also required that a staple be placed every 4½ ft. thereafter.
- When bringing a new wire into any receptacle box, leave at least 6 in. of wire extending out of the box. That 6 in. is a comfortable amount to work with when installing fixtures, receptacles, or switches.
- If you're drilling a hole for a wire through a framing member and the hole gets within 1¼ in. of the stud's surface, be sure to fasten wire protectors (nail plates) over this area, as required by the NEC, to protect the wire from accidental damage during installation of the wallboard or any other type of wallcover.
- If a laundry is included in the bathroom design, the washer will require its own 20-amp circuit. The dryer will require a minimum 30-amp circuit. (Remember, the dryer requires a 240-v circuit.)

TRADE SECRET

An adjustable single-gang box clips on the side of a 2×4 and fastens to the front face with a couple of wallboard screws. This type of box comes in handy when you don't yet know the depth of the finish wall. It's possible, for example, that you have not yet made a final decision on wall tile, which comes in different thicknesses. Once the tile has been installed, box placement can be adjusted to the tile's surface.

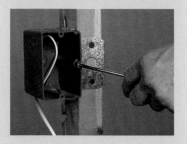

Remove the base molding and cut a small hole in the wallboard near the floor and below your planned electrical box installation. Working carefully through the cutout, drill a 1-in. hole at an angle down through the finish floor and subfloor. Intersect the hole in the floor and subfloor with a new hole drilled from the underside.

When attaching the wire to the electrical fish tape, secure the wire to the fish tape by hooking at least one wire through the eye and overlapping the other wires by at least 2 in. Now tape all the wires together using electrical tape, but do not tape the eye of the fish tape.

Stripping wire cable

I find it easier to strip the jacket off wire cable with a cable ripper before putting the wires in the box, but you can do it afterwards just as well. Be extremely careful cutting the split jacket from the cable with a wire cutter. Make sure that you have only the jacket in the jaws and not one of the wires still in the jacket. If you accidentally cut the

✓ According to Code

Install plastic bushing at the end of rigid conduit (required for a number 4 or larger wire but prohibited for use with NM cable) where it enters a box; this protects the wires from the rough/sharp edge. For armored (flexible) cable, use a fiber or plastic anti-short bushing at the end of the cable (as required by the manufacturer). Slide the bushing over the wires and push it onto the end of the cable.

wires (and if the cable has been cut from the other end), you may have to fish a new cable.

Grounding wire

Now that the cable jacket has been removed, cut the wires to a 6-in. length. Before going any further, use needle-nose pliers to make a loop in the grounding wire to go around the green ground screw. Then use a wire stripper to remove the insulation from the black and white wires to the length recommended on the back of the outlet or switch (usually ½ in.). Be sure to let the wire rest naturally in the opening of the wire stripper as you pull it away from you to remove the insulation. If you twist the tool or the wire, you might nick the wire. Now it is time to move on to the wallboard chapter. This is where it all starts to come together.

The Solderless Connection

Ensure a good connection by using the proper size wire connector for the size of wire you're using. Firmly twist the two wires together in a clockwise direction with a pair of linesman pliers, and snip off any excess wire if the ends are uneven. Place the wire nut over the wire ends and twist the wire connector snugly to create a "solderless connection," and then push the wires and wire nuts to the back of the receptacle box.

For grounding wire, use a green connector (or one with a hole that allows one wire to pass through the hole), thus eliminating the need for an extra pigtail. My favorite wire connector, the ground crimp connector, achieves a solid connection but requires a crimping tool, preferably one that operates from the front nose of the tool. Always leave one ground wire long and then cut off others so as not to overfill the box—nothing is more annoying than working on an electrical box in which someone has cut the grounding wires too short.

Slide the ground crimp connector over the wire and hold it long enough to get the crimping tool around it. Don't let go of the ground wires—then squeeze the crimping tool.

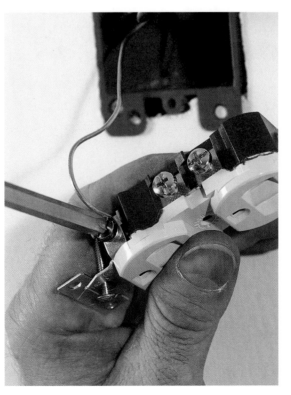

Use a No. 2 Phillips-head screwdriver to tighten down the ground screw. Check to see that the ground wire is secure. Now connect the remaining wires to the receptacle as discussed in the "Receptacles" section on p. 73.

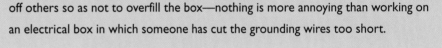

Remove ½ in. of insulation from the wire for attachment to a push outlet, or remove ¾ in. of insulation for attachment to a terminal screw.

Working with

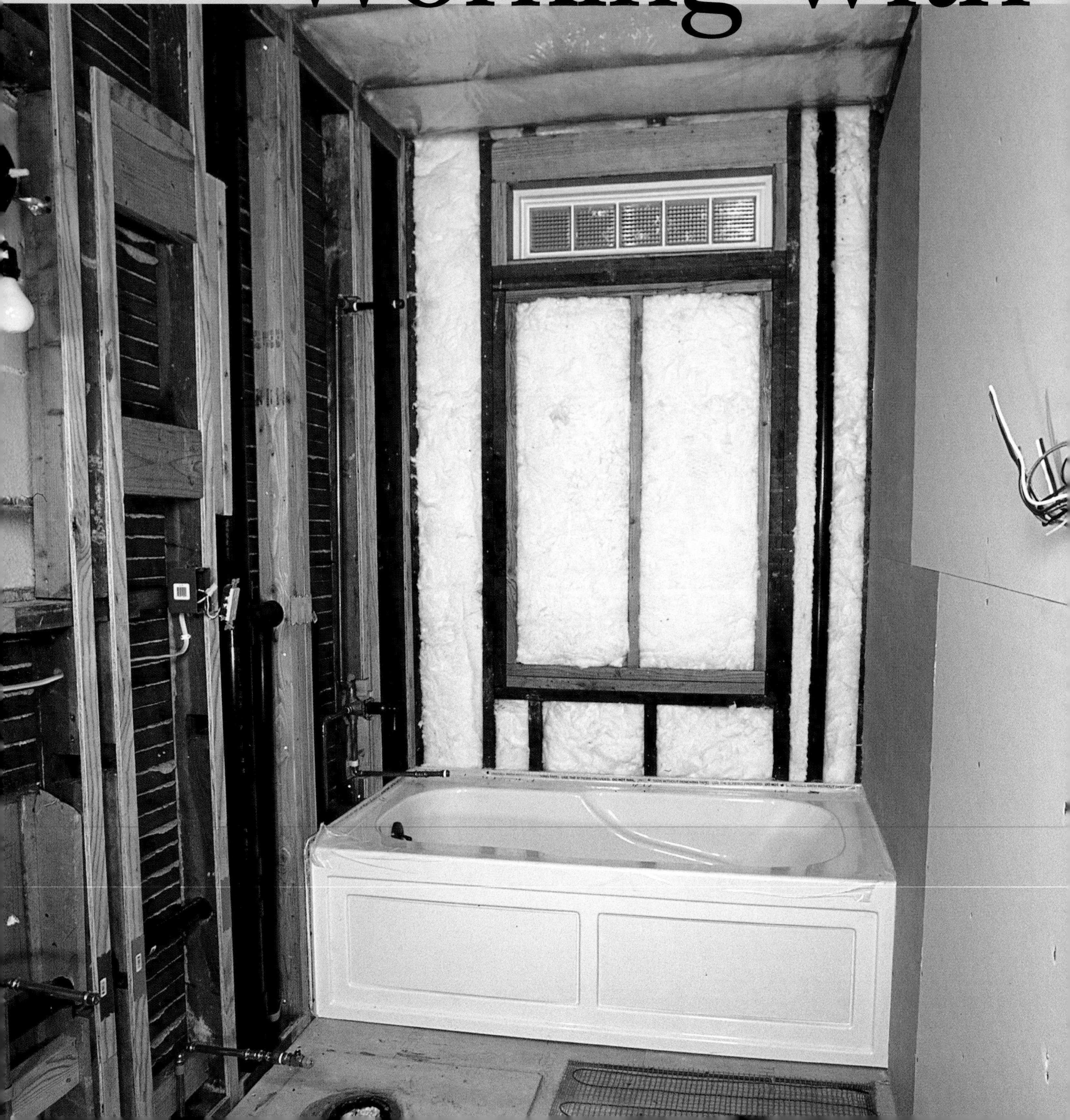

CHAPTER FIVE
Wallboard

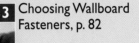
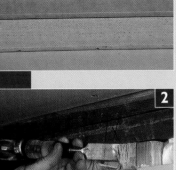

I call this chapter a "downhill" chapter because, now that you've reached this stage of remodeling, it's all downhill from here. In the earlier chapters we focused on the internal systems, such as plumbing and wiring, which make a bathroom function smoothly. Now let's turn our attention to a cosmetic concern: installing wallboard.

Working with wallboard is messy but rewarding work. It requires careful prep, good tools, and the appropriate board and fasteners for your design. It's also helpful to have an extra pair of hands to help hang wallboard and patience when taping the seams.

Because bathrooms are generally small, you'll be able to handle the wallboard work like a pro after reading this chapter. Before you begin, remember to call for final plumbing and electrical inspections. Then, tackle the job with confidence. Out of the dust of the wallboard installation, your bathroom will emerge.

IN DETAIL

Green board is water-resistant, not waterproof, so don't install it in wet areas like the shower. Also, it cannot be used over a vapor barrier, a situation you could encounter on an exterior insulated wall. If your local energy code requires a vapor barrier over exterior wall studs, either use cement board in the shower area up to the ceiling or spread a uniform skim coat of ceramic tile adhesive over the green board where tile or an enclosure kit will be installed and allow to dry before applying the bond coat. Above this area, apply two coats of oil base primer to act as a vapor barrier.

WHAT CAN GO WRONG

In tub/shower areas where the exterior wall has a plastic vapor barrier over Kraft-faced insulation, moisture can get trapped between the face and the vapor barrier, causing mold or mildew growth on the Kraft face and water damage to the bottom plate. Depending on the energy code in your area, you may need to use unfaced insulation in conjunction with an approved vapor barrier.

Understanding Wallboard Products

You'll be using wallboard on the walls and ceiling—and possibly behind the tub enclosure. It's important to select the right type of wallboard for each area—gypsum wallboard, water-resistant wallboard, or cement board—and follow the manufacturers' recommendations for application and installation.

Gypsum wallboard

No matter which wall treatment you plan for your bathroom—paint, wallpaper, or tile—you'll begin with gypsum wallboard. This standard wallboard product is composed of crushed and dried gypsum that is ground to a powder (commonly called plaster of Paris), and then processed and sandwiched between paper. Gypsum wallboard, also known as drywall or Sheetrock®, is not water-resistant, so it's not recommended for use where it might come in direct contact with water.

Like most gypsum wallboard products, standard drywall is available ¼ in. to ⅝ in. thick—the ½-in.-thick board is the most common—and 4 ft. wide. It varies in length from 6 ft. to 16 ft. Each panel's two long edges are slightly tapered so that after it's installed, the shallow recess created at the

Use gypsum wallboard (not green board) for smooth and textured walls and ceilings that won't be exposed to water or long-term moisture.

joint between two panels will accommodate tape and joint compound.

A 4-ft. by 8-ft. sheet of wallboard is too heavy and awkward for one person to handle, so plan to have a helper when moving and installing it.

Water-resistant wallboard

Recognized by its distinctive green face, water-resistant gypsum wallboard, or "green board," is specially processed for use as a base for ceramic or other nonabsorbent finish materials. The gypsum core contains a moisture-resistant chemical, and its multilayered face and back papers are treated to withstand the effects of moisture and high humidity. Similar in construction to regular gypsum wallboard, it's available in the same sizes.

Cement board

Cement board is a lightweight panel composed of aggregated Portland cement and coated with glass-fiber mesh reinforcement. It is resistant to

Water-resistant gypsum wallboard provides a good substrate in the tub/shower area, providing it's not installed over a vapor barrier.

water, moisture, and steam, and it will not decay, warp, or soften. This is the best type of wallboard to use in a tub/shower surround that will be finished with tile. It also makes a strong underlayment for tile floors and countertops.

Cement board panels come ¼ in. to ½ in. thick, 3 ft. wide, and 5 ft. long. They can be scored and snapped, like gypsum wallboard.

✓ According to Code

When considering water-resistant wallboard (green board), check with your state energy code. Installing it on an exterior insulated wall over a vapor barrier may be prohibited.

Fixing Framing Problems

Before you cover up your studs, make a careful inspection. You may find that some framing members protrude beyond the plane upon which your wallboard will be attached. These high spots need to be planed down. Your studs may be bowed, or your ceiling joists may be out of alignment. Now is the time to correct these trouble spots.

Smoothing high spots

Carefully look at the headers above doors and windows. Is the corner of the header extending out beyond the framing stud? Use a chisel or block plane to shave down the high spot. Also, check where studs meet top and bottom plates; chisel off any high spots or file them down using a

A wood rasp helps to remove a high spot on a stud.

IN DETAIL

You may be faced with the problem of filling voids between framing members and wallboard. Fill small voids with a generous application of construction adhesive or nail shims to the framing member. Shims can be purchased at your local home center.

TRADE SECRET

Before installing wallboard, mark the location of framing members on top plates and on the floor. Draw a straight line to denote each framing member's left edge and make an "X" to the right to indicate the framing member's position. Once the ceiling wallboard has been hung, mark the location of the wall studs on it using a pencil. This will help you find the studs once the wallboard is in place on the wall and ready to be fastened.

wood rasp. Inspect trimmers in doorways and around windows. If they stick out farther than studs, consider removing the trimmers to reposition them correctly. If a trimmer is too wide, remove and cut it down to size.

Correcting bowed studs

Make sure you check for bowed studs. One way to detect them is to hold a straight 2×4 horizontally against the wall, with the narrow edge against the frame. Look for gaps between the 2×4 and the studs or for any studs that push the 2×4 out of the wall's plane.

The best way to correct a bowed stud is to cut it partway through (sometimes completely in half), install a wedge, pull the stud in to straighten it, and scab a 1×4 onto each side of it. Ultimately, you may save time by replacing the stud.

Realigning ceiling joists

If you find, after inspecting the ceiling joists, that one is lower than the others, plane the joist until it's even. If you find a joist that curves upward,

attach a furring strip. Finally, watch out for bridging that sticks down farther than the joist. It should be cut flat to the face of the joist.

Choosing Wallboard Fasteners

The following basic information about using fasteners—nails and screws—will guide you in installing your wallboard.

Nails or screws?

All wallboard products can be installed with nails or screws. I use both, depending on the situation. If I've installed a plastic vapor barrier over the studs (and in that case can't apply adhesive), I use screws. When I'm working on the backside of a plaster wall that would probably be cracked if I hammered in nails, I use screws. I also prefer using screws on ceilings. Otherwise, I will hammer nails.

To prevent nails from popping as wood framing shrinks and expands, I use construction adhesive

Here the bridging extends below the floor joist. Most people won't discover this kind of problem until it's too late—that is, when the bridging punches a hole in the wallboard as it's being fastened.

Screws to Use

- When fastening 1/2-in. wallboard to wooden studs, use Phillips or Robinson head #6 or #7 × 1 3/8 screws. Use #6 or #7 × 1 5/8-in. screws for 5/8-in. wallboard.
- Steel studs need self-drilling, self-tapping steel screws, type S for 25-gauge steel framing and type S-12 for 20-gauge framing or heavier. Use 1-in. and 1 1/4-in. bugle-head screws for 1/2-in. and 5/8-in. wallboard, respectively, spacing fasteners 16 in. apart with or without adhesive.
- For cement board, use a Hi-Lo #8 × 1 1/4-in. (or 1 5/8-in.) type screw.
- A fastening schedule for all applications should be checked out with your local building department.

A: #6 × 1 5/8-in. Phillips head
B: #7 × 1 5/8-in. Robinson head
C: #8 × 1 5/8-in. Hi-Lo Phillips head
D: #8 × 1 1/4-in. Self-tapping Phillips head

which also corrects minor framing irregularities. Using both fasteners and adhesive ensures a long-lasting installation.

Apply wallboard adhesive in a bead about 3/8 in. wide and 1/4 in. thick to all the framing surfaces (except the plates) to which the wallboard will be attached. Run a double bead on framing members that back up wallboard joints. If properly applied, the adhesive will be forced out to the edge of the framing as the wallboard is fastened.

If you decide to use nails, use only those designed for wallboard. For 1/2-in. wallboard, use 1 3/8-in. wallboard nails; use 1 5/8-in. nails for 5/8-in. wallboard. Make sure the hammer you're using is a wallboard hammer.

When nailing, start in the center of the sheet and work out to the edges. Always press the wallboard firmly against the framing as you attach it. Drive the nails with the wallboard hammer so the last blow forms a shallow dimple around the nail. The dimple is essential—it's where joint compound will be applied to conceal the nail.

Cutting the tip of the tube properly will help you smoothly apply the correct amount of adhesive to studs.

TRADE SECRET

To get a bead of adhesive that's just the right thickness and diameter for fastening wallboard, cut the tube's nozzle accordingly. The tip on the left is cut for wall installation, while the tip on the right is cut for use in ceiling application.

WHAT CAN GO WRONG

It's easy to install nails or screws improperly. If you miss the nail, fail to hit it squarely, or drive the screw in too far, you're likely to tear the wallboard surface paper. Using the wrong type of screw altogether is also a common problem. It's not too late to correct the situation—drive another fastener 2 in. above or below the first one.

Fastening schedule. Space fasteners according to a fastening or nailing schedule that's appropriate to your specific application. Your building department may include this schedule as part of its code, so check with them before getting started.

Nails. When nailing a ceiling without adhesive, space your nails no farther apart than 7 in. On sidewalls, nails should be no more than 8 in. apart. Nail between ⅜ in. and ½ in. from the edge of the wallboard panel.

When using adhesive on framing members spaced at 16 in. or 24 in. on center, space nails 24 in. apart in the field of both ceiling and walls. Nails at the edges and ends should be fastened 16 in. apart.

Corner beads. Drive nails opposite each other and no more than 9 in. apart.

Screws. When using adhesive and working with framing members spaced 16 in. or 24 in., drive your screws 24 in. apart except at edges and ends, where they should be fastened 16 in. apart.

If you are not using adhesive, place screws 12 in. apart on ceilings and 16 in. apart on sidewalls, assuming framing members are 16 in. on center. With water-resistant wallboard, the screws should be spaced 12 in. apart on both ceilings and walls. If you plan to apply tile to water-resistant gypsum wallboard, the screws should be no farther than 8 in. apart. Again, check with your building department for their recommended spacing. Remember, green board can't be installed on ceilings where the framing members are spaced more than 12 in. apart.

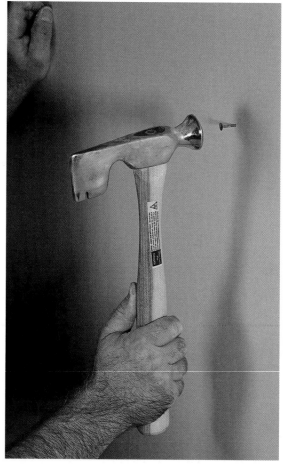

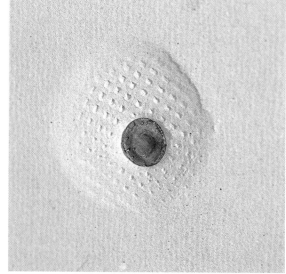

Making a dimple with the proper depth, like the one shown here, ensures adequate coverage with joint compound.

A wallboard hammer has a specially designed head that creates a proper-sized dimple.

Hanging Wallboard

There are a couple of rules to follow when installing wallboard. First, always begin with the ceiling, and then move to the walls. Second, plan your panel layout to minimize the number of 4-ft.-long butt joints between panels. The ultimate goal is to use the maximum length of a sheet.

To save time and improve the finished appearance, plan your drywall panel layout on paper. Drywall panels are long enough (and most bathrooms are small enough) so that it's possible to have panels run from wall to wall with no 4-ft-long butt joints in the middle of a wall or ceiling. If an end-to-end joint is unavoidable, make sure that it's staggered, or offset, from another joint. Butt both ends together over a framing member.

To help lock the framing members together and create a secure framing system, wallboard should be mounted so it spans across the framing members on both ceilings and walls.

Ceilings first. Measure the wallboard and score the finish side with a utility knife, using a T-square as your guide. Bend the panel back, and then cut through the paper from the back to separate the pieces and prevent the paper from tearing. Smooth the ends with a wallboard rasp, if necessary. With a helper, fasten the wallboard in place across the framing members and against the wall studs.

Walls. Install wall panels across framing members beginning at the top. Butt the top edge of the wall panel up against the ceiling drywall. It is important to have a helper who can hold the wall panel up against the ceiling while you drive the fasteners. I recommend that you butt two wallboard edges together before installing fasteners because it's easy to damage an exposed edge with a hammer or by driving screws too close.

When installing water-resistant wallboard, keep the factory edge up off the tub or shower pan about ¼ in. On the remaining walls, remember to

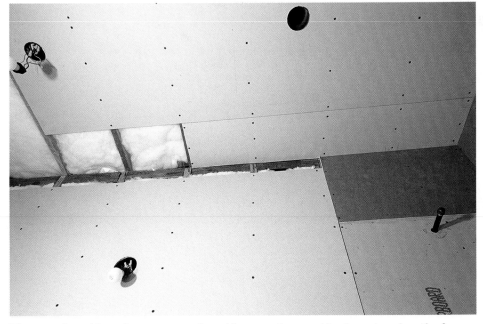

Tie green board into the gypsum rock, making sure the panel lands centered on the framing members.

Interior Corners—To Float or Not to Float

Some contractors feel that partial nailing along an inside corner where wallboards meet, called a floating interior corner, is a good way to avoid surface cracking caused by everyday structural stress. They recommend holding back ceiling nails 7 in. to 12 in. from the wall, and sidewall nails 8 in. to 12 in. down from the ceiling.

I prefer to take extra precautions during the framing stage in order to secure the wallboard completely at the corners and to minimize the chance of structural movement. First, I don't use green studs for framing because they will shrink far more than kiln-dried framing lumber and increase the chance of drywall cracks and nail pops. Second, I allow materials to acclimate to room temperature for about a week. Finally, I make sure that whenever a framing member rests on or against another one, it's completely nailed—when a joist rests on a double plate, for instance, or where walls come together. Having taken these precautions over the years, I've yet to experience stress or surface cracking.

cut out holes for outlet boxes and any other fixtures beforehand. Transfer the measurements to the wallboard and cut using a keyhole wallboard saw. A saw like the Rockeater can cut a punchout for a water line as small as ½ in. in diameter. Remember to cut from the finish side and as close

PRO TIP

Don't force wallboard into place. If the fit is too tight, shave the edge using a wallboard rasp; joint gaps should not exceed 1/16 in. to 1/8 in.

IN DETAIL

Your plumbing manufacturer will provide you with a faucet template to trace around during wallboard installation. To avoid cutting the plumbing pipes, remove the wallboard, cut out the traced area with a keyhole wallboard saw, and then install and fasten the wallboard. Don't throw away the template. It will come in handy to cut tile or, if you're installing a tub/shower enclosure kit, the wall panel.

TRADE SECRET

Do not "float" wallboard. Mount backers where there is no framing member so you secure each panel around its complete perimeter. For example, wherever a wall runs parallel with upper and lower framing members, a backer board, like the 2x4 shown here, is nailed onto the top plate.

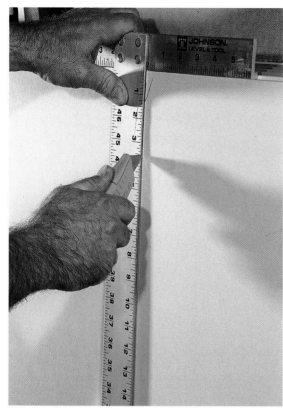

Keep your hand on top and your foot up against the bottom of the T-square to hold it in place as you cut.

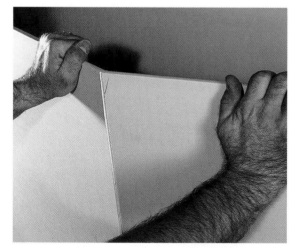

Secure the larger part of the wallboard with one hand and use the other hand to push back on the smaller piece to snap the wallboard at the score line.

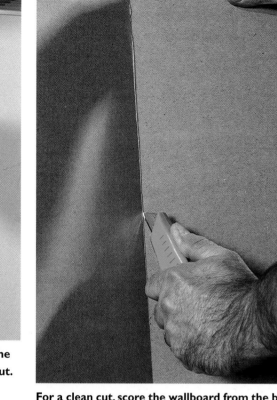

For a clean cut, score the wallboard from the back with a utility knife.

If the sheet doesn't break cleanly, use a drywall rasp to clean the edge.

to fixtures as possible so there are no gaps when you install the finish trim.

For the plumbing wall, fit your wallboard before cutting the holes for the showerhead and tub spout. If your wall is out of square, your cutouts may be off. Cut holes just large enough to go over the stem assembly. The faucet housings and pipe escutcheons (or any finish trim) should cover the gypsum wallboard or tile behind them. Be sure to caulk cut edges and openings around pipes and fixtures with a flexible water-resistant caulk or adhesive to prevent any water from getting into the backside of the wallboard.

Continue your wallboard installation, cutting carefully around door and window openings,

If you're working alone, position a flat bar (as shown) on the floor underneath the wallboard; step on it to lift the wallboard up against the bottom edge of the top piece for fastening.

Corner Bead Made Easy

Once the wallboard is in place, install corner bead over all outside corners. You can use tape-on corner bead, which is embedded in joint compound and put on when you are taping, or you can use nail-on metal corner bead, which I think yields a corner that's less prone to cracking.

When installing metal corner bead, use the maximum length whenever possible, because piecing lengths of corner bead together is tricky. Take a window, for example. Work on the top and bottom pieces first. Be sure to notch both ends of the flanges to create wings that extend beyond the window opening the same distance as the flange width (roughly 1/8 in.).

Before you cut the side pieces, securely nail the top and bottom bead in place using drywall nails in the prepunched holes. It's important to allow the corner bead to rest naturally against the corner. Do not to push in on the bead and change the manufacturer's profile. Properly installed, the bead will extend slightly beyond both the wallboard outside corner and its own flanges, thus creating a bed to accommodate your compound.

Check your installation by placing a straightedge or the edge of a taping knife on the wall, extending it out beyond the corner bead. If the corner bead is correctly in place, the straightedge will touch only the outermost tip of the bead and there will be a void between the knife edge and the wall. Your taping knife will be guided by that corner tip as you apply joint and finish compounds.

To install the side pieces, cut, notch, and trim the flange using either a 45° or 90° angle (as shown) to overlap the flanges of the previously installed corner bead. Again, secure both side pieces, including its ends, and remember not to push in on the bead.

The metal corner bead flanges have been notched for installation over the top and bottom corner beads.

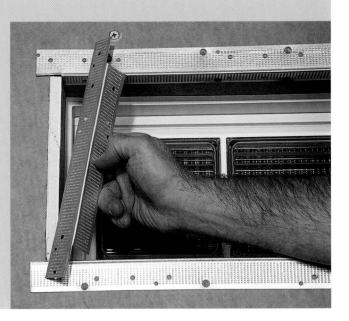

IN DETAIL

If you have installed a whirlpool-type tub, you will discover that the tub has an approximately 1 in. by ¼-in.-thick flange around it used to secure the tub to the back and side walls. Install wallboard up to this flange but not over it. However, the flanges that run down the front sides of the tub that fasten to the sidewalls are too wide and deep to accept a mud and tape filling. Instead, attach ¼-in.-thick backer board over the flange with screws and tape it properly. Finish this area like the rest of the walls to ensure a smooth, even surface for tile or trim.

Slide the faucet template over the stem assembly and trace around it. Depending on its design, you may have to turn the template around to get a clean tracing edge.

plumbing pipes, and other places, such as a laundry drain or water supply box. Check to make sure that you're not breaking through the surface of the paper as you drive the nails and screws into the wallboard.

Once the wallboard has been hung, it's time to tape.

Taping

Taping is a challenging part of the project. Understanding the products and tools involved is the first step in achieving successful results.

Getting started: joint compounds

You'll need two kinds of mud: all-purpose joint compound (or taping compound) and topping compound. Both come premixed in buckets and boxes. Purchase one of each in 5-gal. buckets and any additional compound in a box. When the bucket is empty, clean it completely before dumping a new box of compound into it.

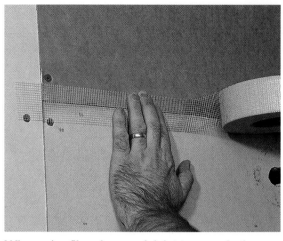

When using fiberglass-mesh joint tape, apply the tape before the mud compound.

You will need wallboard joint tape that's made of either paper or fiberglass mesh. The paper tape, used by many professionals, is preferable, but if this is your first time taping, you might find the fiberglass tape with its pressure-sensitive adhesive backing easier to use. This tape is pressed onto the wall without using any joint compound, but it is finished in the same fashion as paper tape.

Joint and topping compounds are premixed, but stir them before use with a ½-in. spade-handle drill set on a slow speed. Hold the bucket securely between your feet so it doesn't spin. Before you apply compound, carefully add a little water to loosen it but be careful not to overthin it. Dip a wallboard finishing knife into the compound to check its consistency. The mud should stick to the knife's blade, and when you tip the blade, the mud should slide slowly toward the edge of it without falling off.

Tools

You'll need a 12-in. mud pan for holding the joint or topping compound, a 4-in. knife for the first coat, a 6-in. or 8-in. knife for the second coat, and a 10-in. or 12-in. knife for the third coat. To make taping easier, purchase a tape holder that houses both the mud pan and tape. It keeps everything at your fingertips and speeds up the taping process. An inside-corner tape creaser is also handy. For sanding, you'll need a pole sander for the upper walls and ceilings, and a hand sander for inside corners and the lower walls.

Applying compound

Applying compound is a tedious and messy part of the job, so I suggest that you follow these steps with extra care. Professional tapers might take a different approach, but I've found that my method neatly conceals all cut tape ends and yields smooth joints.

Joint compound. Dip the knife into the pan at an angle and load only half of the blade. Next, draw the blade out over the metal edge of the mud pan to clean the backside of the blade. For

With the right products and tools, taping wallboard joints can go very smoothly.

best results as you apply the compound, use medium pressure and hold the knife at a 45° angle.

Begin with the short vertical joints. Using a 4-in. blade, apply an even, thin coat of compound along the entire length of the joint. Center the tape over the joint at the top and lightly press it into the compound with your fingers. Then, starting again at the top of the joint, draw your blade

Place your index and middle finger on the backside of the blade to help stiffen and control it.

WHAT CAN GO WRONG

If the compound oozes out from under the tape or the tape folds in on itself, apply less pressure with the finishing knife as you smooth the compound over the joint.

TRADE SECRET

The key to applying topping compound successfully is to alternate the second coat so you do not overlap wet applications. For instance, if you are applying compound to an inside corner, do one side only. On the other side, apply compound on a horizontal joint over to the next corner on the other side of the wall. You should be able to alternate the second coat all the way through the job. Once the first side of each of the inside and outside corners and joints has dried, apply topping to the sides of the corners that were not done the first time around, and work through the job alternating applications as before.

Always start at the top of vertical joints and draw the knife downward with even pressure.

At the ceiling line the tape is being embedded into the joint compound.

down firmly over the tape to embed it in the compound. Be sure there's sufficient compound under the tape to prevent it from blistering. If this should happen, lift the tape with the corner of your knife and reapply compound. While drawing your blade over the tape, remove excess joint compound from both edges so you have a smooth surface for the second coat.

Allow your first coat to dry for at least half a day before you tape the horizontal joints. As you work on these joints, overlap the pieces of tape where they intersect with the previously applied vertical strips.

Next, tape the inside corners, beginning with the horizontal corners. Using your 4-in. knife, apply compound to both sides of the corner from wall to wall. Fold the tape along the center and lightly push the crease into position with your fingers or the 4-in. knife. Embed the tape and remove any excess compound, just as you did with the other joints. Be careful not to cut the tape fold with your blade.

Wait until these corners dry for a day before you apply tape to the vertical inside corners. Start at the ceiling and apply compound and tape down to the floor. This is a good time to spot, or apply mud, to the heads of the fasteners.

Topping compound. When the joint compound is dry, it's time to apply the first coat of topping compound. First, carefully scrape off imperfections with your 4-in. knife. Check inside and outside corners and fasteners. Even out high spots with 100-grit paper. Stir the topping mix and apply compound with the 6-in. or 8-in. knife to horizontal joints, corners, and fastener heads. Use the 10-in. or 12-in. blade on vertical joints. Spot the fasteners again. For the second coat of topping compound, repeat the steps, spreading the mix over a larger area and feathering the edges.

Check that all dried, taped joints are level with the surface of the wallboard by holding a 12-in. blade across a vertical joint perpendicular to the wall to see if the blade "rocks" from side to side. If it does, apply compound to both sides of the tape, feathering it with an 18-in. blade. Achieving a smooth, level surface might take five or six coats.

Once the last coat of topping compound is dry, scrape and sand any bumpy areas. When you are satisfied, wipe the walls with a damp sponge to remove any dust.

Finishing Wallboard

In this final stage, we'll look at the various ways of finishing your walls—making them smooth or textured, painting them, or covering them with wallpaper. Each of these finishes requires a different surface preparation, but none is too tricky to master.

Smooth

If you plan on a glossy paint finish, you'll need a smooth surface, which involves a little extra prep. Consider applying a skim coat, or thin layer, of topping compound, to seal the wallboard paper. After the skim coat, the walls or ceiling surface should be lightly sanded or sponged.

Instead of a skim coat, apply a third coat of topping followed by a latex base primer, an option I prefer. If this first primer coat raises wallboard paper fibers, you might see imperfections that were not noticeable before; a light sanding with 200-grit to 300-grit paper will knock down the rough patches. Check for smoothness, wipe off any dust, and prime these areas again. Once the walls are dry, you are ready to apply your finish paint.

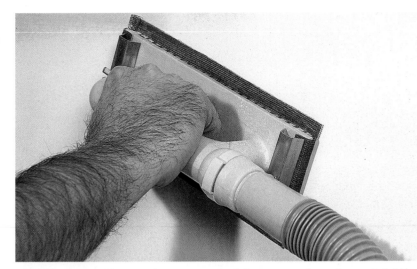

This dust-free sander attaches to a wet-and-dry vacuum for a cleaner job. Use a vacuum with a double filter and an extra hose to vent the exhaust through a window.

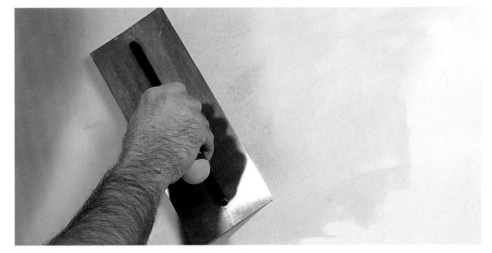

A finish trowel is used to apply the skim coat.

Textured

If you are interested in a textured finish for your wall or ceiling, you can opt for a number of looks. The three most popular textures for wall applications are orange peel, splatter, and knockdown. You can purchase premixed textures or mix your own, and you might even want to create your own pattern. First you'll want to choose the degree of your texture—from coarse to fine. Ceiling and wall textures are sprayed on with a hopper that uses air pressure or with a hand-held pump-spray gun. (You can rent the hopper and compressor from a rental center.) You can also roll texture on or knock it down (spray on the texture

✚ SAFETY FIRST

When spraying wall or ceiling texture in a confined area, pay special attention to the location of the hose and the compressor. It's very easy to trip over the hose or to step back onto the compressor and lose your balance. If at all possible, keep the compressor out of the room that you're spraying.

PRO TIP

To avoid sanding over fastener spots, use a damp sponge to feather the dried compound into the wallboard surface.

TRADE SECRET

Take care not to sand a groove into corners. If you are using sandpaper designed for wallboard, remove the ear on one side to prevent the problem.

IN DETAIL

If you are not completely sure whether or not you want textured walls, prime them first and apply the texture to a small area only; you'll have less to remove if the effect is not what you want. Use the widest taping knife you have to scrape the texture from the walls. When most of it has been removed, use a warm damp sponge to wipe off the rest. Be careful as you scrape not to damage the wallboard. Remember that primer will still be required over the texture even if the ceiling and walls were primed first.

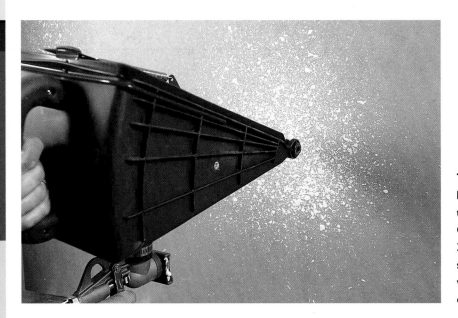

The fully enclosed hopper on this pattern pistol gun by Goldblatt permits 360° spill-free spraying—it's great when you're working on ceilings.

then flatten it with a wallboard knife). Before spraying anything on the wall, practice with the equipment. Experiment on a scrap of wallboard until you find a texture you like.

Paint

When preparing new walls for paint, begin with a primer coat to achieve a uniform finished appearance. (You'll also want to use two coats of primer on the tub/shower walls where you plan to use tile or an enclosure kit, even if the wallboard is water-resistant.) Without primer, no matter how many coats are applied, the finish paint will be absorbed at different rates on new wallboard and on the compound used to tape the joints, resulting in a hi-lo effect. You can use polyvinyl acetate (PVA) primer to seal wallboard, but I prefer to use enamel undercoater or Zinsser's Bulls Eye® water-base primer-sealer and stain killer followed by a latex semigloss paint for the finish. Flat paints do not wash easily and are more subject to wear. For smooth and textured walls, I recommend painting with a ½-in. or ¾-in. nap lamb's wool roller. These rollers hold a lot of paint and distribute it evenly, yet with a slight texture, on the wall surface.

Remember to read and follow the manufacturer's instructions, and work in a well-ventilated

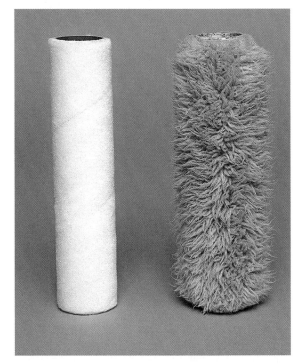

The lamb's wool roller (on the right) is more than fifteen years old, but it just keeps getting better. The synthetic roller (on the left) costs less but may shed synthetic fibers.

room. Always apply two coats of finish paint, and be sure to paint far enough into the tub or shower area so you won't have any touching up to do when tile or the tub/shower surround is installed. Be sure to allow at least the recommended drying time between coats and before you attempt to install any fixtures, outlet covers, and adhesive for tiles or for rubber or vinyl cove base molding.

Wallpaper

The best wallpaper for bathrooms is solid vinyl, which is durable and easy to maintain. Another type, vinyl-coated wallpaper, comes in a range of patterns, but its backing tears easily compared to the solid vinyl variety. If you select easy-installation prepasted wallpaper, you'll want to use wallpaper adhesive (paste) with it because of the bathroom's high moisture level.

Purchase enough wallpaper for the entire job, because dye lots or print runs can vary. For that reason also, check each roll before you start to work to make sure that the patterns and colors match. Your dealer will have specific recommendations on how to prepare the walls. In most cases, the best method is to seal new wallboard with PVA primer or paint it with an oil-based topcoat, and then apply sizing. Zinsser®'s Prepz® combines sizing with an adhesive activator and is formulated to work over painted walls and vinyl wallpaper.

Now that the walls are done, we can move on to flooring, cabinets, and countertops.

Textured Finishes: From Orange Peel to Crow's Foot

- **Orange Peel.** This finish can be applied in heavy, medium, and light textures. Use a compound no thinner than the consistency of latex paint. Set the compressor to a minimum 60 psi to 80 psi.
- **Splatter.** Similar to orange peel, splatter is often used to cover wall defects. It requires a heavier mix (less water) with the compressor set at 45 psi minimum.
- **Knockdown.** Knockdown is an appealing texture but harder to achieve than orange peel or splatter. After spraying on the desired texture at 45 psi, wait 10 to 15 minutes for the compound to set up. Using a flat blade, very lightly flatten only the surface of the spatter. Always start at the top, pull as low as you can reach, and then come up from the bottom, keeping the pattern going in one direction.

    For ceilings, consider textures such as skip trowel, swirl finish, or crow's foot. Choose ceiling and wall textures that complement each other.
- **Skip-trowel.** Skip-trowel is achieved by applying the mix by hand or by spraying the compound at low pressure to create larger spatters. When applying the compound by hand, add 2 cups of clean silica sand to the mix. The sand allows the knife to skip across the surface, which emphasizes the effect. In a spray application, wait 10 to 15 minutes for the compound to set up, and then knock down the spatters, applying more pressure than you did for the knockdown pattern.
- **Swirl Finish and Crow's Foot.** Completely wet the paint roller's ¼-in. to 1-in. nap with the mix, then apply it to the surface as evenly as possible. When it has dried to a dull wet finish, move across the surface in a circular motion with a wallpaper brush to achieve the desired swirl texture. For the Crow's Foot pattern, substitute a texture brush and press a little harder. Once the texturing is completely dry, prime the walls and apply your paint.

A thicker mix makes deeper patterns; a thinner mix makes flatter ones. Higher pressure yields smaller patterns, as shown on the left; less pressure yields larger patterns, as shown on the right.

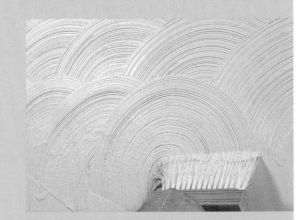

This swirl pattern is a great look for a ceiling with crown molding.

Flooring, Cabinets,

and Countertops

Floors, cabinets, and counter-tops define major design elements of your bath. This is a critical stage in the job because now the decisions made earlier about patterns and color schemes all come together.

Whether you've picked vinyl sheet goods or ceramic tile, flooring makes a strong first impression. Cabinets, prebuilt or custom-made, can create stylish and attractive storage while the right countertop can add unique personality to your bath.

If you've made it this far, give yourself a pat on the back. Thorough preparation is crucial, so I encourage you not to rush through this stage but to work carefully to achieve a professional finish. You'll see that these procedures are much less involved than anything else we've covered up to this point, and chances are you've had some experience with installing at least one of these components.

PRO TIP

Before installing cement board, wipe both sides with a damp sponge to remove dust. Rewipe outer surface before applying thinset.

WHAT CAN GO WRONG

When you're installing fasteners in Hardibacker, be aware that its extremely hard surface might cause screw heads to snap off. Another potential problem is the dulling of a countersunk bit. To prevent either of these things from happening, first drill a pilot hole with a ⅛-in. bit, and then use Hi-Lo screws (see p. 83 in Chapter Five).

IN DETAIL

Plywood underlayment should be fastened with screws because nails are more likely to work loose as the wood expands and contracts. If you discover that nails were used to attach your existing underlayment, drive a deck screw within 2 in. of both sides of each old nail.

Available underlayment products include Hardibacker (left), exterior grade plywood, good on one side (center), and cement board (right).

Underlayment Issues

Before installing a new floor, it's important to make sure the underlayment is structurally sound, smooth, and clean.

Underlayment for resilient flooring, usually plywood, should be free of depressions or foreign deposits because these irregularities will eventually telegraph through the new flooring. Also, if the surface is dusty and dirty, you won't achieve the proper bond between underlayment and the finished floor. For a ceramic-tile floor, you'll need a substrate like cement board that won't flex when the floor is walked on—flexing can cause tile and grout lines to crack.

Plywood underlayment

For vinyl or other resilient-finish flooring, use plywood approved for underlayment installation. Your local lumber dealer can recommend the appropriate grade. Don't use particleboard as an underlayment—it swells when it comes in contact with water over time.

While your subfloor is exposed, check the nailing pattern to determine where the floor joists are

Avoiding Asbestos

If your current floor covering contains asbestos, you might be able to bypass expensive removal and disposal procedures by installing new underlayment and floor covering over the existing asbestos product. Before you do this, check with your local Environmental Protection Agency (EPA) office to make sure it's acceptable practice.

For a new floor, ⅜-in. underlayment is generally appropriate, but a thinner underlayment may be needed over an existing asbestos floor to achieve a good match-up with adjacent flooring. Fasten the underlayment with adhesive and ring-shank nails or screws. Don't forget to check to see if you can open and close the door. The toilet flange or the wax bowl ring may need alteration for proper installation of the toilet.

located and mark joist locations on the walls near the floor. Then lay 15-lb. or 30-lb. roofing paper over the subfloor. This serves as a vapor barrier and helps prevent squeaky floors. It can also work to even up new and adjacent floors.

Installing underlayment. When installing underlayment, make sure the sections run in the same direction as the subfloor and overlap all sub-floor joints by a minimum of 2 in. For those joints that land between two joists, I recommend that you either extend the underlayment to the next joist or hold it back to the previous one—you want to be able to anchor the joint to a solid framing member.

If possible, position underlayment joints in the center of a framing member. Also, avoid having a joint in the high traffic area in front of the thresh-old. Arrange the sections of your underlayment so that a solid, unjointed piece fits in the opening.

When installing the underlayment, loosely butt the ends, and stay about $\frac{3}{16}$ in. away from the walls and tub/shower. If you choose to nail down your underlayment, use a ring-shank nail that is long enough to penetrate the floor joists at the joints, and to go at least $\frac{1}{2}$ in. into the subfloor in the field. I prefer to fasten the entire underlayment to the sub-floor using $1\frac{1}{2}$-in. deck screws by driving the screws' heads just below the surface of the underlayment.

When attaching $\frac{3}{4}$-in. underlayment, you should normally space screws 4 in. apart around the perimeter and along the joints, and 6 in. apart in the field over the floor joists.

Drill for the toilet flange, if necessary, and fill all screw holes, gouges, gaps, chips, sunken edges, and joints more than $\frac{1}{4}$ in. wide with a quick-setting, nonshrinking filler compound such as Durham's® Water Putty. Sand out any imperfec-tions and sweep or vacuum the area, making sure that all dust is removed from the plywood sur-face. Before laying the finish floor, check the underlayment one more time for any imperfec-tions you might have overlooked.

Proper Placement of Plywood Joint

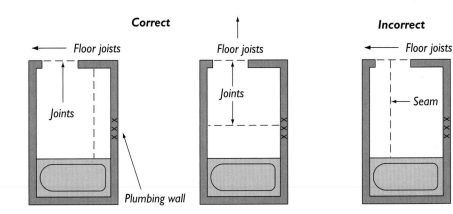

Correct joint placement for plywood underlayment, or any other underlayment product, is a must for a stable substrate.

Considering a Concrete Subfloor

If your new bath is in the basement, it's likely the subfloor is concrete. Before laying flooring over it, the surface should be dry, smooth, structurally sound, and free of depressions, scales, and any types of cleaning agents.

Concrete subfloors, particularly those less than two years old, should be checked for high moisture content. To test for moisture, tape a 2-ft. × 2-ft. section of clear plastic or aluminum foil to the concrete slab, forming an airtight seal. Wait 24 to 48 hours and check under the plastic or foil. If you find condensation or discoloration, the moisture content is too high.

You should also conduct a bond test. Remove any oil, grease, paint, varnish, or other surface treatments, and then install a small section of flooring, at least a 36-in. square. This test should be conducted at temperatures of at least 50°F.

You can plan to install your flooring if the patch is securely bonded after 72 hours or if an unusual amount of force was needed to lift the patch from the surface and you notice adhesive clinging to the backing and the concrete. (Be sure to scrape off the adhesive from these test areas with a razor scraper before you install your flooring.) If the material does not adhere tightly, you have a moisture problem, and you'll need professional advice.

A dusty or chalky surface should be swept clean, vacuumed, and sealed. This condition may be a sign of alkali salts, so first test for alkalinity. The pH on the sur-face can be determined by slightly wetting the floor and applying pH test paper. (A range from 6 to 8 is acceptable.) Balance the surface pH with an alkali-neutralizer product to promote adhesion or consult a professional.

Use the flat side of the trowel to spread the thinset firmly into the substrate, and then use a ¼-in. notched trowel to comb it to the correct thickness.

IN DETAIL

If the flooring you're installing calls for ¼-in. plywood underlayment, consider one of the new underlayment systems. Fabricated with marine-grade adhesives, these products will not warp, buckle, or delaminate. They feature a preprinted "X" nailing pattern on the top surface. Choose an underlayment product that meets your flooring manufacturer's specification; your dealer can help you select one. These new products, however, are not recommended for use with ceramic tile.

Cement board

When installing a tile floor, use cement board as the underlayment. Before laying cement board over an existing subfloor, be sure to check that the subfloor is solidly fastened.

Begin by applying a setting bed of latex-modified mortar over the plywood subfloor using a notched trowel. Next, while the mortar is still workable, fasten the cement board every 6 in. to 8 in. over the entire area with Hi-Lo screws.

Make sure that the joints do not line up with the joints of the subfloor. Allow approximately ⅛ in. spaces between panels and, using a flat-edge trowel, fill them with the mortar. It is not necessary to tape these joints, but taping does provide a flat, uniform surface. If you decide to tape, use a fiberglass tape. Remember, always check the subfloor- and floor-manufacturers' specifications before getting started.

Laying Down Flooring

The floor is the first thing you see when the bathroom door opens, so choose your material carefully. Almost any covering—vinyl, ceramic tile, carpet, or even wood—will work. Vinyl flooring, is easy to install and maintain, and it holds up well to water. More costly ceramic tile takes effort, but it creates a clean, formal look. Carpet and wood work—if they're not in contact with water. Whichever flooring you choose, consider maintenance, style, installation, and cost.

Tile is durable, especially with a cement-board underlayment and well-maintained grout.

Vinyl flooring

Vinyl, or resilient, flooring is a moderately priced, water-resistant material that comes in two types: tile or sheet. Vinyl tile comes in 12-in. by 12-in. or 9-in. by 9-in. squares; some are backed with self-adhesive and others require glue. Vinyl tile, especially residential peel-and-stick tile, does not work well in a bathroom environment because the seams leave it vulnerable to water and dirt. Sheet flooring, with either a printed pattern or inlaid colors, usually comes in 6-ft.-, 9-ft.-, or 12-ft.-wide rolls. Unfortunately, some types of sheet flooring can tear or dent, and imperfections in the underlayment below it will show.

Printed-pattern floors are comprised of a backing material, a layer of foam cushioning, the printed pattern, and a protective, clear, wear layer. When this type of flooring is installed, seams between the sheets are sealed using a special solvent that actually welds the two pieces together.

The pattern on inlaid-color floors is built up by fusing thousands of colored vinyl granules with heat and pressure. Then a wear layer is applied. This process gives a rich look to the floor and results in a material that's highly resistant to dents, tears, and gouges. Because it's stiff and difficult to work with, manufacturers recommend professional installation.

Installing a sheet vinyl floor. The key to a successful installation is cutting and fitting the vinyl. There are two ways to proceed: by using the freehand "cut-and-fit" method (the one I used in my bathroom) or a template.

Making a template. If this is your first time working with vinyl, I recommend that you make a paper template, or pattern, from building paper that you've cut to fit the shape of the room. It's fine to create your pattern from several pieces of paper; just make sure to tape them together. While you're cutting out the pattern, make triangular holes in the paper every 2 ft. to 3 ft. so you can tape the template to the underlayment as you work and keep it from shifting. Then, when the template is complete, lay out the vinyl on a flat surface and tape the pattern to it. Keep in mind that you can move the template around on your sheet vinyl to find the design layout for the room. Finally, when you're satisfied with the way it "fits," trace the outline of the template onto the vinyl with a grease

Rubber base molding will cover the grout lines close to the wall.

PRO TIP

When choosing resilient flooring, consider location, maintenance, the type of underlayment you'll need, cost, and installation.

IN DETAIL

A warranty should add to the value of the floor you are considering. Knowing what a floor warranty covers can prevent costly surprises. Read each flooring manufacturer's warranty carefully and get answers to the following:

- What is the length of the warranty after installation and under what circumstances will the manufacturer replace or repair the floor covering?

- Does the warranty cover wear, loss of gloss, or discoloration?

- Does the floor covering have to be installed by a professional in order to be covered?

TRADE SECRET

To squarely place a vinyl grid floor pattern, line it up in two high-visibility areas: along the tub and in front of the doorway. If the grid lines run parallel to the tub and the door, your floor will look fine.

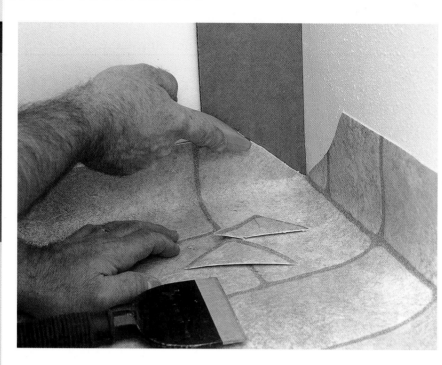

When making corner cuts, protect the wall with ⅛-in. hardboard or a piece of plastic laminate with the finish side out.

pencil, and then use a straightedge and cut just outside the line with a utility knife.

Using the "cut-and-fit" method. Roll out the floor covering in the bathroom. It will curl up at the sidewalls in the shape of a "U." Now carefully cut the vinyl at the walls' inside and outside corners so the floor covering lays freely up against the walls. Take care not to cut into the curled portion of the vinyl. Next use a stiff straightedge to push down on the floor covering where the wall and floor intersect (the "U"). Apply pressure to the straightedge and cut the vinyl with a utility knife. In small bathrooms I prefer to use a 4-in. brick chisel instead of a straightedge. Take your time and make small cuts as you go, and be sure to use a sharp blade in your utility knife. Dull blades can tear the flooring material.

Applying mastic. Once you've cut the floor covering to size, you are ready to apply mastic. Begin by laying out your flooring material, then roll half of it back. Sweep or vacuum the underlayment and the backside of the vinyl. Check the label of the mastic for the recommended trowel size. Spread adhesive on the

cleared half of the floor, and then roll the covering onto the mastic. Next, roll back the other half of the flooring beyond the area just glued down. Again, sweep or vacuum the underlayment and back of the vinyl. Now trowel mastic onto the clean, exposed underlayment, overlapping the mastic you previously applied.

Use a roller to smooth the floor covering, working from the center of the room to the perimeter. Your goal is to force out any air bubbles trapped underneath. Finally—and this is very important—seal the edge where the flooring meets the tub or shower pan with painter's blue masking tape. This will keep dirt out until you are ready to apply the appropriate caulk.

Tile flooring

Tile is the most popular nonresilient flooring choice. It can easily withstand water, steam, and constant humidity. Installing tile is more involved than laying a vinyl floor, but it provides an attractive, long-lasting surface that's well worth the extra effort and cost.

Glazed tile with a slip-proof matte or textured finish is a smart choice in the bath. Mosaic tiles,

Two Sides of Vinyl

- **Finishes:** When considering vinyl flooring, remember to think about the wear layer—whether it's vinyl or urethane. A factory-applied wear layer essentially replaces the need for wax and dramatically reduces the time spent on floor care. Both urethane and vinyl wear layers protect the color and pattern of the floor, and they are stain-resistant. Urethane is a lot harder and will keep its like-new appearance longer. It also offers a glossier shine and tougher scuff resistance. A vinyl wear layer loses its luster sooner, but it can be polished.

- **Backing:** Resilient-floor backing also varies from product to product. Perimeter-installed floors, which are attached to the underlayment only at the perimeter, have a flexible, tear-resistant backing that stretches over most floors and underlayments. Vinyl with PVC backing can be installed as a floating floor or full spread (also called a "glue down"). It, too, is flexible and less prone to moisture staining—it's a good product to use in a basement bathroom as a loose lay (i.e., without glue). Felt-back floors need to be glued entirely using mastic.

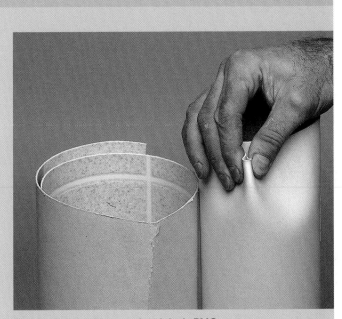

The flexible backing on the right is PVC—stronger than felt (on the left) and more resistant to moisture, stains, and dents.

Properly troweled mastic should show the grooves.

TLC for a New Vinyl Floor

If you're installing a new vinyl floor, keep the following in mind:

- For the first 24 hours, do not walk on the floor, especially if there are seams.
- For at least two days, keep the room temperature at 68° F or greater to allow the adhesive to set up properly.
- For at least a week, do not wash the floor.
- If your new vinyl floor is in a bathroom/laundry room, allow the adhesive to set up at least a week before bringing in any appliances.
- Immediately cover any cuts or gouges in the vinyl flooring with packing and/or painter's blue masking tape, and then call a floor-covering professional. A repair may be possible, but dirt or moisture in the cut or gouge will make it difficult to repair correctly.

PRO TIP

Glossy, smooth, or plain vinyl flooring shows irregularities and stains much more than patterned and matte surfaces do.

TRADE SECRET

Use a 4-in. Marshalltown® brick chisel to push down on the floor covering and into the wall-floor intersection at the same time. Cut with a utility knife on the wall side of the chisel and continue the process along the length of the wall.

WHAT CAN GO WRONG

Poor installation or the improper type of underlayment can cause seams in resilient vinyl flooring to separate. If a seam begins to split, fix it immediately, before dirt and water get underneath. As a temporary measure, cover the seam with packing and/or painter's blue masking tape. Reseal the seam using the product and technique recommended by your flooring's manufacturer—epoxy applied to the underside, for example.

Glazed floor tiles don't absorb water.

because of their additional grout joints, provide a less slippery surface, too.

Installing a Tile Floor

Before you can install your tile floor, you must make sure that your subfloor is level and firm enough to handle the weight of the tile. A springy floor will crack tile, so if the floor needs stiffening or leveling, shore up sunken areas and fill irregularities by applying a quick-setting, nonshrinking leveling compound. Then cover the subfloor with at least ⅜-in.-thick exterior grade plywood, approved ¼-in. underlayment, or (preferably) ¼-in. to ½-in. cement board. (Take note that if you're planning to install base cabinetry, this is the time to do it, after installing the underlayment.)

Finicky Flooring: Hardwood and Carpeting

Water will destroy hardwood and carpeting in any bathroom. If your space is large enough or configured in such a way that tile or vinyl can be installed in the tub/shower area, then wood or carpet might work in the rest of the bathroom.

If you've got your heart set on installing hardwood, finish it with a marine-type varnish. Also consider laminate flooring, or even engineered-wood products, which are more suitable here than hardwood. They are made of wood strands, veneers, lumber, or other forms of wood fiber that are bonded together to produce a composite material. You still won't want to install these products in wet areas.

If you decide on carpet, keep it out of wet areas as well, or consider an outdoor carpet with a moisture-resistant backing made of closed-pore vinyl or latex foam. On a concrete basement floor, consider water-resistant, rubber-backed carpet that has a nonskid backing.

Hardwood should be installed only in dry areas of the bath.

As long as it's in a relatively dry location, carpet can add some comfort to your bathroom. Consider a loose-fit for easy air drying.

Next, do a dry run by laying the tile out on the floor. When you're satisfied with the layout, pick up the tile, and then clean and dry the underlayment surface. Next apply thinset adhesive, and seat the tile according to the detailed instructions I give in Chapter Seven. After the thinset is adequately cured, fill the joints with grout.

Installing Cabinets

Prebuilt or custom-made—both of these cabinetry options have their pros and cons. Prebuilt units tend to cost less, but they don't have the look and feel of a custom-made cabinet, and because of their standard configurations, they may not fit your space. Custom cabinets are likely to be more expensive and take time to craft, but you'll be getting a piece that best suits your bathroom's space and style. For example, a standard-depth prebuilt cabinet over the toilet will look out of proportion, but one that's custom made—in a depth ranging

This 5-in.-deep cabinet was custom built. The detailed crown mounted at the top gives it dimension and helps tie it in with the crown molding at the ceiling.

Tools and Tips for Cabinet Installation

Tools and Hardware

The tools you will need to install upper and lower cabinets include:

- Handsaw
- Drill and countersink bit
- Screw gun
- Tape measure
- Level
- Hammer and rubber mallet
- Trowel
- Pry bar
- Two C clamps
- Carpenter's square
- Stepladder
- Stud finder

Here's the hardware you'll need:

- Screws with coarse threads (1⅝ in. to 3 in. long)
- Finish nails (brads)
- A putty stick that matches the finish
- Toggle bolts (used to fasten to wallboard when you are unable to fasten to a stud)
- Adhesive as recommended by the cabinet manufacturer
- Wooden shims (used to level base and wall cabinetry)

Helpful Tips

- Remove doors and drawers before installing cabinets.
- Drill pilot holes for your fasteners.
- Use a countersink bit for drilling stiles or back upper rails.
- Use clamps when installing cabinets side by side.
- Use cardboard or a piece of wood at both ends of the clamp to protect the face-frame edges.
- Whenever possible, conceal installation screws behind hinges.

IN DETAIL

Keep these measurements in mind as you select cabinets:

- A washbasin requires a minimum 24-in.-wide vanity.

- A bathroom cabinet is 33½ in. high (without the top) and 18 in. or 21 in. deep.

- In a barrier-free bathroom, the washbasin must be installed a minimum of 29 in.—and no higher than 34 in.—from the floor, as measured from the underside of the washbasin. This allows knee space for a wheelchair user. The washbasin cannot be deeper than 6½ in., and it must measure a minimum of 11 in. from the front of the drain to its front edge. The washbasin must extend at least 17 in. from the wall.

TRADE SECRET

Use a right-angle drill to fasten a base cabinet to the floor at the ends of the toekick; the area doesn't leave much room for working with conventional screw guns.

from 4⅝ in. to 8 in. will be more in balance. Also, if your prebuilt cabinet has come from the factory with simulated wood-grain sides, you can conceal them with finish panels that match the front of the cabinet. These finish panels can be purchased from your cabinet supplier.

Try not to locate a cabinet too close to a wet area like the tub. It can be difficult to clean up water in a tight space, and the moisture can ruin the cabinet's finish. It's best to keep the vanity at least 6 in. away from the tub—that gives you enough room to wipe up any excess water. If space is limited, install a smaller-width vanity with a premolded washbasin, available at your local home center.

Preparation

Cabinets must be plumb and square for their drawers and doors to function properly. The first step is to use a straight length of 2×4 and a carpenter's level to check the floor and walls in the cabinet area for high spots. When you locate the highest point on the floor, measure and mark a level baseline on the wall near the high point to indicate where the top edge of the base cabinet will need to fit. Also lightly mark the outline of your cabinet on the wall to check its placement against your layout. Locate studs so you can fasten the cabinet to them when securing it to the wall.

Installing upper cabinets

Install recessed medicine and upper cabinets first, beginning with the upper corner cabinet (if you have one). Measure up from the floor baseline to mark the baseline of your upper cabinets. It helps to have a second pair of hands (or a T-brace made from rough lumber) to support the weight of the cabinets as you install them.

Make sure screws are long enough to hit either backing or a framing member. Carefully fit and glue prefinished panels to upper cabinets to conceal the simulated woodgrain sides. You can drive ½-in. brads to hold a finish panel in place while the glue sets. Make sure to countersink the brads and camouflage the holes with a matching putty stick.

Leveling the floor in both directions beforehand eliminates problems as you install the base cabinet.

Backing installed during framing (plus a cabinet stand) made installing this custom-made cabinet easy.

Installing lower cabinets

A 5-ft. by 9-ft. bathroom will probably have a base cabinet with a sink and side drawers, and most likely the cabinet will be installed in the corner. If your unit is prebuilt, it may have the back removed to allow for plumbing. A cabinet with a solid back, usually one that's custom-built, will require holes to be drilled for plumbing lines.

At this stage it's important to check the level points of the cabinet—both parallel and perpendicular to the wall. This will help you to correctly position shims, if you should need them. When fastening the cabinet, start at the back wall, not the sidewall. Install the fastener through the solid back if your cabinet is custom-made and through the back upper rail if the cabinet is prebuilt. This

Level the cabinet both parallel and perpendicular to the wall before fastening it in place.

Drill pilot holes before installing fasteners, especially if you're using a shim.

When fastening the cabinet to the floor, use a long screw, drill a pilot hole, and position your screws close to the floor so they'll be covered by the base molding.

WHAT CAN GO WRONG

The back wall where you're installing your base cabinet may be bowed or have irregularities. If you try to attach the rail directly to it, the cabinet will be thrown out of square and doors and drawers will not function properly. An easy solution is to install shims on the back rail to compensate for any wall irregularities.

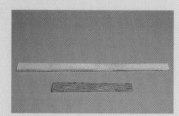

IN DETAIL

Shims are key when it comes to installing level cabinets. Doors and drawers open and close with ease when your cabinet is level. You may need to place shims under the toekick—and on the sides and back of the cabinet—to make it level. You can make your own shims, but it's cheaper and easier to purchase them at your local home center. They are available in two handy sizes: mini and extra long.

will allow you to shim the front of the cabinet under the toekick.

Cabinets are fastened to the floor through the side panels near the toekick with 2½ in. screws. Predrill no matter where screws will be fastened through the cabinet. The toekick of a prebuilt cabinet is very thin, so if you plan to attach the cabinet through the toekick, install the fastener close to the side panel. Attach the cabinet to the sidewall into solid framing members and trim all shims.

If the cabinet has a side finish panel, scribe the panel and cut it to fit with a hand saw. You'll need to cut out for the toekick and cut out the toekick's overhang on the cabinet.

Installing Countertops

You can add a lot to the look of your bath with the right countertop, whether you choose one made from plastic laminate, tile, granite, marble, concrete, or a man-made solid surface like Swanstone®.

Plastic laminates and tile are somewhat easy to install, but man-made solid surfaces and natural stone have to be fabricated and installed by factory-authorized pros. These countertops take time to produce, so it's important to account for this in your work schedule.

There are many types of countertop materials and numerous ways to construct a countertop, but here I'll discuss a plastic laminate top with a wood front edge in detail. Our granite countertop is briefly discussed on p. 108.

Starting with the substrate

You can purchase a prebuilt countertop, complete with backsplash and no-drip front edge, that's made from plastic laminate and MDF substrate. Alternatively, you can attach MDF substrate (available in 25-in. widths) to the cabinet and glue plastic laminate onto it to create your own finished platform for the sink.

To make your own countertop, fasten ¾-in. furring strips across the top of the cabinet with screws to provide a mounting surface for the substrate and to raise the countertop so its 1½-in.-thick edge will not interfere with the operation of a cabinet door or top drawer.

Cut the substrate material to size, keeping in mind that the recommended overhang for a finished countertop is 1 in. If the factory edge is clean, keep it to the front and position the cut side to the wall. If you are planning a plastic laminate edge, use a softwood. If you're opting for a hardwood edge to match your cabinetry, then cut the countertop overhang back to ¼ in. The addition of ¾-in.-thick softwood or hardwood will bring the overhang out to 1 in. Fasten the countertop material to the furring strips attached to the top of the cabinet, countersink the screws, and putty the holes.

For laminate tops, it's OK to overlap the softwood edge for an outside corner. Hardwood finish edges, however, require mitered outside corners for a neat appearance. To attach the ¾-in. by 1½-in. softwood or hardwood edge, glue it to the edge of the countertop material with yellow wood glue and countersink the finish nails deep enough to hold putty.

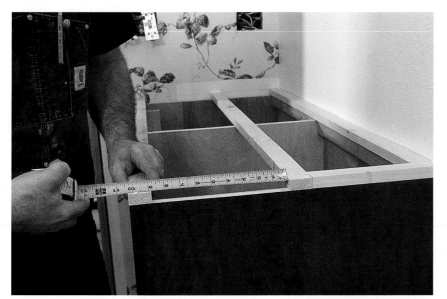

To add height to the counter, attach furring strips to the top.

Check as you work to make sure the wooden counter edge is even with the surface of the countertop substrate. To ensure tightly mitered corners, apply pressure to the edge pieces when predrilling, sink your nails, and be sure to use yellow wood glue. If you're attaching a hardwood edge, take care not to get any glue on the surface. If this should happen, quickly use a clean, white rag and warm water to wipe off any excess. Once the edge is complete, use a finish sander to go over it, then dust thoroughly.

Installing plastic laminate

Plastic laminate needs to be cut and fitted for a trial run before gluing. Measure the countertop and add about ½ in. to both length and width; this will give you enough material to work with if your wall is out of square. Using a carbide scoring tool and straightedge, score the face of the laminate several times until you have removed enough material to snap it apart.

Do a trial fit and mark the sink cutout. When you're happy with your laminate's measurements, it's time to glue it to the substrate piece. This process involves applying adhesive to the substrate, and then to the underside of the laminate. Use a laminate roller to ensure that the adhesive completely covers

Make sure glue completely covers all but the sink-cutout area.

each surface, but do not apply contact cement to the sink area. Use a disposable drop cloth underneath the laminate while applying the contact cement.

Old venetian blind slats that have been adequately cleaned can be used to help hold the glue-coated laminate up and off the glue-covered countertop until the laminate is correctly positioned. After the contact cement has dried for the recommended time, spread the slats out over the countertop, convex-side up. Carefully place the laminate in

PRO **TIP**

Before installing plastic laminate, remove any tape and lay it flat for a few days at room temperature.

IN DETAIL

To cut laminate, use a carbide scoring tool, a straightedge, and a scrap piece of laminate to catch the blade as it comes off the end. Apply pressure to the straightedge as you notch the laminate—use your knee for added pressure. Draw the tool toward you, scoring the finished side at least three times. Continue to apply pressure to the straightedge while you quickly lift up the free side of the sheet—the laminate will break with a snap.

IN DETAIL

Creating an invisible seam in plastic laminate can be achieved but it is time-consuming. You can use seam filler—available in a range of colors—as a last resort to fill any voids between pieces of laminate. Experiment before using it, follow the manufacturer's instructions, and clean off any excess with solvent. Work quickly—this product dries very fast.

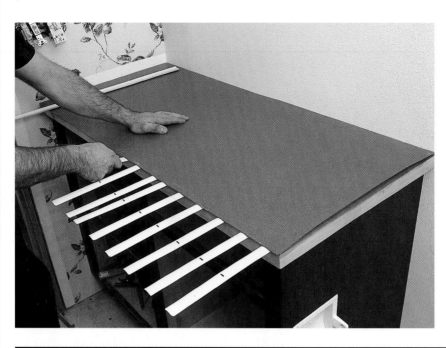

Working from the wall out, pull out the slats one at a time and apply pressure to the laminate as you work—without getting too close to the next slat in line.

The Grand Look of Granite

The granite countertop, nicely complemented by a self-rimming undermount sink, is held in place with sealant and wooden blocks.

A stone countertop with rich aesthetic appeal and organic beauty can bring character and personality to any bathroom—for a price. If you've chosen one for your bath, take into account the weeks it could take for the counter to be delivered and installed. Stone countertops should only be put in by authorized factory fabricators and installers.

Our fabricator explained to us how a granite top is made and installed. The most important step is selecting the raw stone—one side of which is already polished. The next step is to choose an edge profile. Then an installer will make a hard template and, back at the shop, cut the stone to size. After the edge is polished—or laminated, if that suits your bathroom's design—cutouts are made for the sink and faucet. Finally, the top is ready for installation.

position—the slats will keep it away from the contact cement until final adjustments are made.

Working from the wall out, remove a few slats and press the laminate down onto the countertop. Be careful not to press too closely to a slat or you won't be able to pull it out. I find that working about 2 in. away from a slat will do. Using an extension roller, continue to press the laminate down onto the countertop, applying firm, even pressure. Make sure you roll over all areas of the laminate, paying special attention to the edges, to ensure a tight bond. This job has to be done right the first time, because the glue is unforgiving. Once the surfaces come in contact, they bond instantly.

The final step is to rout the edge, trimming off the ½-in. excess with a router or laminate trimmer equipped with a carbide bit. Periodically check the roller on the router bit for contact cement buildup. The cement buildup will burn the face of the counter edge. A standard router won't work against the wall or in small angles, so use the laminate scoring tool and a 12-in. straightedge. Take your time and work very carefully so the underside of the laminate doesn't get chipped or break out. A disc sander can be used to remove most of the remaining material. Select at minimum a 3-in. disc pad; it should extend out beyond the side of the drill by an inch. You could also trim away the excess carefully with a sharp chisel or file.

To finish up the edge, use a flat file with a fine pattern. Then switch to a hand sanding block with 100-grit sandpaper to smooth the edge where the laminate meets the wood. When you are satisfied with its smoothness, apply finish to the wood surface.

You may be eager to drop in the sink, but the next phase is to install the tub/shower enclosure.

A trimmer or router should be used in a counter-clockwise direction.

In the sink area, drill a hole in the center of the laminate that's large enough to fit the router bit comfortably. Before turning on the router, make sure the bit is not in contact with the sides of the hole.

Tub and Shower

CHAPTER SEVEN
Enclosures

Your tub/shower enclosure, or surround, has to withstand the punishing effects of hard water, soap scum, and shampoo. The tub/shower is probably the most-used item in a home, so it's important not to use lesser quality products or take shortcuts with its installation.

Tub enclosure kits come in sizes, shapes, styles, and colors to fit virtually any design. Some kits are very easy to install, while others may require professional installation.

There are several challenges you may encounter when installing a tub/shower enclosure. The walls may not be true, the tub may have settled, or the kit pieces may be out of square. Don't worry. There are solutions that will still result in a quality installation. In this chapter I'll show you how to install a solid surface tub enclosure kit and offer some pointers for fiberglass kit installations.

PRO TIP

Install a ready-made access panel through the backside of the wall so you can later change the valve of your new tile or fiberglass surround.

TRADE SECRET

Before installing a tub/shower fiberglass wall enclosure kit, grind off any imperfections around the edge on the backsides of the panels.

TRADE SECRET

The "Shower Tower®" by Swan is a fiberglass unit that allows valve replacement while maintaining the surface of the existing wall. This single piece comes preplumbed (for a standard or hand-held shower head) and in bone or white.

About Bathtub Wall Enclosures

You can buy a bathtub wall panel system kit (or surround) made of PVC, fiberglass, or solid surfacing material, among others. Wallboard, plaster, and painted walls all make appropriate substrates, but avoid using existing tile as a substrate. My kit installation instructions should be used as a basic guide; be sure to follow the manufacturer's instructions to protect your warranty.

Tub/shower solid panels

A typical kit is designed to fit different-sized tubs and showers. Most include panels with or without corner inserts, shelving for soap and shampoo (if not built into the panel), color-matched silicone sealant, caulk, and a roll of pressure-sensitive tape.

The pressure-sensitive tape on the back of the panel is extremely sticky, so take care not to touch it.

The unit I installed in my bathroom, a Swanstone® solid-surface surround, has matching accessory items.

To install the panels you'll need a jig saw, drill, tape measure, straightedge, level, caulking gun, adhesive, caulk, pressure-sensitive tape (if not provided), and tools to install the tub/shower door.

Putting in a tub/shower surround.
Before you begin, take care to protect your tub/shower surfaces. It's also easy to mar the surround kit surfaces when making cuts, so cover the bottom of your jig saw's foot with masking tape.

Level the panels and mark both vertically and horizontally on the walls with a pencil where the panels will be installed. Always cut the bottoms of the panels to fit squarely on the tub, and level at the top (for both back and sidewall panels). Measure carefully, support the panels, and cut using a jig saw. Always trial fit your panels, especially those with pressure-sensitive tape on the back. It's nearly impossible to remove a crooked panel to straighten it; you really have only one opportunity to mount a panel correctly.

If you're installing a fiberglass kit, apply latex caulk with silicone or a polybond tub-and-tile-adhesive sealant in every place where panels overlap. Do the same for trim pieces that overlap joints in solid surface materials. If caulk isn't included with your kit, purchase the type recommended by the kit manufacturer and select a color that matches the unit.

+ SAFETY FIRST

To avoid getting fiberglass splinters, be sure to wear gloves when handling any fiberglass tub/shower wall enclosure kits or surrounds. Also, wear a mask to prevent inhaling fibers.

Use blue painter's masking tape to mark the cut for a recessed accessory shelf and to protect the surface from the base of the jig saw.

Level the top of the back panel. Cut the bottom so the side panels meet it level at the top and evenly on both sides.

The back wall goes on first. In a solid surface application, trial fit the back wall. If you have a fiberglass kit with corner panels, trial fit them first. The corner panels should go in vertically with a loose-to-snug fit to the sidewalls. Also, make sure they're level at the top, cut to sit squarely on the tub, and ready to receive the back wall panel.

Plumb sidewall panels are essential. Use a level on the outside vertical edge of the sidewall panels. If your panels lean toward the back wall, then plumb them, mark them at the bottom where they meet the tub, and cut them off so they drop to the tub squarely. Using a compass with a pencil, vertically scribe the inside sidewall panels where they meet the back wall. Use a jig saw to make a uniform cut, so the sidewall panels fit snugly up to the back wall panel.

Making sure that the surround is plumb all the way around the tub and that the panels match evenly at both ends of the tub will give you a pro-looking installation. If the panels are uneven, it will be obvious once the shower door—which also must be level—is installed.

If you put the panel in straight and the tub is crooked, you'll have a noticeable gap at one side

To trial fit the plumbing sidewall panel, use a hole-saw to cut openings just large enough to fit over the plumbing. Depending on the depth of the 90° drop elbow for the showerhead, the hole can be cut with the side panel in place.

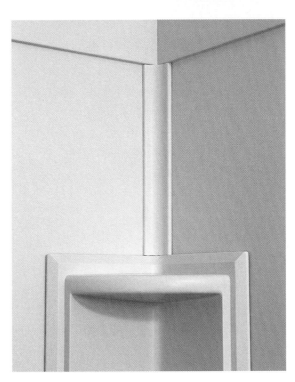

If your enclosure comes with inside cove molding, first caulk the inside corner and allow it to set up for 24 hours. Then cut, fit, and install the molding for a finishing touch.

PRO TIP

Before installing tile, remove protruding objects—fixtures, baseboards, nails, screws—and loose or damaged plaster, wallpaper, paint, or grease.

IN DETAIL

When purchasing tile, be sure it comes from the same production run, and check for uniform color and texture. If the dealer doesn't have enough tile from the same run and recommends a partial order to complete your project, order instead the amount of tile it will take to install the entire project, including extras. You might want more tile if you have an additional project in mind, or you may have to replace damaged tiles.

IN DETAIL

To learn more about other tile and grout applications, contact the Tile Council of America, Inc. (www.tileusa.com), for their Handbook for Ceramic Tile Installation and other printed materials. There is a small fee for the information they provide, however, it's well worth the price.

Window Treatment

A window in the shower area needs special attention. If the window is high enough, it can be cased out in water-resistant wallboard, also called green board. Otherwise, use 1/4-in. cement backer board, and then install tile on the sill and both jambs. For a unified look in our bathroom, we chose a Swanstone window-trim kit to match the tub enclosure kit.

You can install window kits with mitered joints or butt joints, as shown. To prevent standing water, shim the sill near the window so the front tips slightly downward.

of a panel when you apply caulk, so you might have to "fudge" your level a little bit to ensure that the panels match evenly at both ends of the tub.

After you have applied the adhesive, rest the panel on the edge of the tub. Press firmly from the bottom up, keeping the top of the panel away from the wall until you gradually work your way up to the top. There's no room for error at this stage.

Installing Tile

There's a reason ceramic tile is such a popular choice for the bath: it's easy to install and it looks great. With product innovations like thinset adhesives, special trim pieces, and easy-to-use grouts, even beginners can get professional results. Installed correctly and maintained on a regular basis, ceramic tile will last forever.

The basics of tile installation

The basic method of installing tile is the same regardless of the surface—countertop, floor, tub/shower, or walls. What differs is the substrate, or backing, and the type of adhesive used. Contact your local tile dealer for recommendations.

On the sidewall, begin the first course with the outside corner and bullnose tiles.

Tiling a tub/shower surround. Before spreading the first trowel of mastic, decide if you're going to tile just the tub/shower area or continue your tile outside the tub or shower pan. If you plan to continue the tile field, decide how wide it should be. (It's usually as wide as a bullnose tile.) Next, draw a vertical line as far from the edge of the tub as the width of the tile you've chosen. You'll be setting the tile to just cover that line.

When determining how high your tile will be, begin with the plumbing wall. Choose whether or not you're going to install tile above the

Tile Essentials

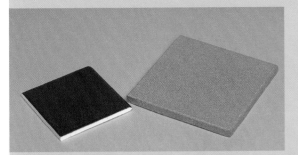

Notice the differences between the glazed ceramic wall tile on the left and the unglazed quarry floor tile on the right.

A grout coordinated with your tile can enhance the look of your bath.

As you shop for tile, you'll discover that there are four main tile categories: glazed ceramic wall, paver, quarry, and ceramic mosaic. Quarry, paver, and ceramic mosaic come in both glazed and unglazed finishes. The glazed ceramic tile has a glass-like surface that can be shiny, matte, or textured. High-gloss tile is generally used in areas where scratching is unlikely to occur, such as walls or tub/shower enclosures in bathrooms. The ceramic-tile category also includes glazed floor tiles—matte or textured—many of which have a rustic stone look.

Unglazed quarry tile develops a natural gloss as it ages, giving it a soft shine. It also maintains its natural color, which runs throughout the body of the tile. Unglazed mosaic, paver, and quarry tiles are more durable, so they are commonly used for floor and outdoor applications.

While most tiles can be installed on walls, countertops, bathing platforms, showers, tub enclosures, and floors, it's important to use tiles that are recommended for a particular use by the manufacturer.

Selecting the correct grout—the material used to fill the spaces between the tile—is just as important as the tile you choose. Grouts are available in a variety of colors that can be used to coordinate or contrast with tile colors, and they can be modified to provide specific qualities such as whiteness, mildew resistance, uniformity, hardness, flexibility, and water retention. Portland cement is the base for most grouts, but a latex additive can speed up the curing time and help the grout spread more easily.

showerhead. If you decide to stop tiling below it, make sure the tile ends just beneath the flange of the shower neck. Once you determine where you want the tile to stop, draw a horizontal line around the perimeter of the tub/shower area.

Next consider the bottom row of tiles, which actually sits just off the tub or shower pan. Using individually cut tile in this row will allow you to make minor adjustments if the tub/shower has moved out of plumb during installation or if an existing bathtub has moved as the house has settled. Make sure to adjust the overall height of the tiles so that the cut tile for the bottom row is more than half a full-size tile's height. However, don't cut within ½ in. of the tile's edge. Tile edges are very hard, and making this cut is very difficult unless you're using an electric tile saw. I find that a

A vertical pencil line guides tile placement on the sidewall.

IN DETAIL

When a laminate vanity countertop requires a tile backsplash, always start with an outside corner and work toward the inside corner. A simple approach would be one row of bullnose tile and the outside corners. To create a more interesting backsplash, use a row of field tile split in half, add a row of 1-in. × 8-in. rope wall accent tiles above the field, and then top it off with a row of bullnose tile.

cut of about 1 in. from the tile's edge works well and gives the best overall final appearance. When cutting the tiles remember that you'll want to leave about a ¹⁄₁₆-in. gap between them and the bathtub or shower pan. Use 80-grit sandpaper and a hand-held sanding block to knock down the face edge of each cut tile. The gap will be sealed later with caulk.

Setting tile. Once you've mapped out your tile, the next step is applying mastic. In doing this, make sure you have a V-notched trowel with the proper-size notches, usually ³⁄₁₆ in. wide by ⁵⁄₃₂ in. deep. Read the instructions on the back label of the can of mastic for specific dimensions. Apply the mastic to a small area so that you have time to attach the tiles before the mastic sets up. Also, when applying adhesives, keep them below the top row by about ¼ in. That will prevent the adhesive from oozing out and onto the wall when you set the tile.

After the mastic is spread, start setting tile (bullnose), in the center of the top row, normally starting with the back wall. To seat each tile, press the tile firmly into place with a slight twist. Work your way out from the center in both directions and down the wall.

Align the tiles, both bullnose and field, so all joints are uniform and straight. If you are using self-spacing tiles, the tiles will have lugs or knobs on the edges that will automatically space the

Apply the mastic using a trowel appropriate for the tile being installed.

The cardboard underneath this portable manual tile cutter protects the floor.

Plumbing Wall Particulars

The plumbing wall requires patience and more time to complete than the head side-wall because there are obstacles to cut around—the showerhead, valve, and tub spout. Don't attempt these cuts without specialized tile tools.

Avoid splitting tiles as you cut them to fit around the plumbing hardware. By taking your time as you cut, you can make it look as though you never cut the tiles at all. There are three ways to accomplish this: use a carbide ceramic hole saw with a drill, a carbide rod that fits in a hacksaw, or tile nippers. Nippers come in handy when you only have to nip off a small piece. Be sure to use only tools designed for cutting ceramic tile. If you have to drill a hole near the edge of a tile, take care that you don't break the tile.

A carbide ceramic hole saw cuts a clean hole. Drill from the finish side; wear eye protection.

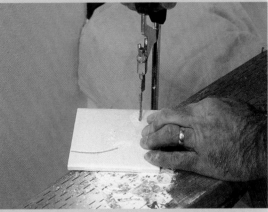

When making a cut this large, use a carbide rod and go halfway from one side, then start again from the other.

Cut the tile carefully around the plumbing fittings for a professional finish.

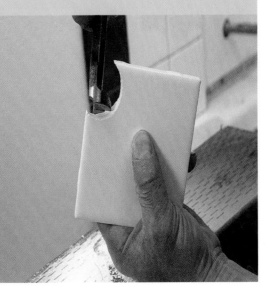

Carefully clean the cut with nippers.

117

PRO TIP

Experiment with your tiles and projected pattern by laying out a dry run of the tiles on the countertop's substrate.

IN DETAIL

One way to make a bathroom look rich is to install a tile countertop. Use cement backer board as an underlayment over a minimum ½-in. plywood substrate—or follow the manufacturer's specifications. In the dry run, lay out the tiles so that the cut ones will be up against the wall; they'll be less noticeable that way. If the counter has a washbasin, work from the sink edge outward. Otherwise, start in the center. If the countertop is between two walls, make sure that both end tiles are cut to approximately the same size.

TRADE SECRET

Normally it's easier to remove and replace both tile and grout, but there's no reason to replace tile just because of grout problems. Also, replacing tile may not be possible if the project involves historic restoration and the tiles are no longer available or cannot be affordably reproduced. Grout removal is a painstaking process with a hand-held tile grout saw, but Grout Grabber in a reciprocating saw will speed the process tremendously. Some handwork will still be required, though.

If the piece is tight, don't force it into the corner; cut another one instead.

Here tiles need to be cut to fill in around the soap dish. It looks better if the tiles are cut equally.

Secure the soap dish for at least 24 hours using blue painters' masking tape.

grout joints, but you should still check to make sure the joints are indeed evenly spaced—just one oversized or undersized tile could throw the joints off. If you are not using self-spacing tiles, purchase tile spacers to achieve even grout lines.

Check periodically for loose tiles by pushing on one corner of a tile. If the corner sinks in and the opposite corner pops out, you didn't apply enough mastic. After cleaning off the tile and wall space, apply sufficient mastic to the tile and reseat it.

The general rule of thumb is to set at least three or four rows of tiles before cutting any tiles to complete the row. Slightly knock down (using 80-grit sandpaper and a hand-held sanding block) just the face edge of any cut tiles that butt into existing tiles in a corner. Allow a ¹⁄₁₆-in. gap between these tiles. Tiles cut using the snap-and-score method (manual tile cutter), normally don't make a clean break so you'll need to sand off the irregularities and bevel the top edge. This sanding technique and very small gap will produce a clean visual edge under a thin bead of caulk (to be applied later).

Always cut the smallest corner piece first (whether it's the back or sidewall) and then butt the adjacent piece against it. Once the back wall is complete, tile the sidewalls.

When you reach the second or third row up from the tub, decide where to install a soap dish.

+ SAFETY FIRST

Soap dishes with a built-in washcloth holder, towel holders on shower doors, and a towel bar just outside a shower are not designed to be secure grab bars, and they should not be used as such—serious accidents can happen. Plan ahead when framing to provide secure backing for a standard grab bar in an area that will be convenient.

The best location is on the back wall, away from the plumbing wall and out of the path of the spray. If you're installing ceramic tile, use a ceramic—not metal—soap dish. You can glue the soap dish with mastic and complete the tile installation, including cutting in the last row. Or you can leave the spot uncovered, and then come back and install the soap dish using clear silicone. Remember that a soap dish, especially one with a washcloth holder, really doesn't have support behind it, so it won't carry much weight.

Applying grout. After the required setting-up time has passed, usually 24 hours, it's time to grout. If you've used caulk in the joint where the finish flooring meets the tub or shower pan, apply a protective strip of masking tape over it before getting started.

Mix the grout according to the manufacturer's instructions, adding powder to liquid little by little. Stir the mixture manually until the grout powder is uniformly wet. Let it stand for about 15 minutes, remix, and use it immediately. The grout should be free of lumps. When scooped from the bucket, it will hang onto a rubber grout float yet still be thin and creamy enough to be squeezed into the joints.

Start with the head sidewall. Use a rubber grout float at a 30° angle and spread the grout diagonally across the joints, spreading only as much as you can handle comfortably—4 sq. ft. or 5 sq. ft. Once the grout is spread, go over the area a few times with a side-to-side motion until the joints are packed, and scrape off the excess grout with the edge of the float.

Take a clean wet sponge and thoroughly wring it out. Then wipe over the tile and remove any grout standing on the surface. Clean the sponge often and sponge the grout off the walls right away. Don't make the mistake I made on the first tile job I got when I went into the business over twenty years ago. I grouted the entire tub/shower

Work grout into all joints using a rubber grout float.

Take care not to apply too much pressure on grout joints as you clean the tiles.

area, and because it was almost lunchtime, I went to lunch. About an hour later I returned to clean the excess grout. Five hours later, I was finally finished—just about the time the customer was coming home.

For uniform grout lines, let the area you've just cleaned sit for about ten minutes while you clean another area. Return to the first cleaning site and, using hardly any pressure, wipe quickly over the grout lines with a damp sponge—first horizontally, and then vertically. Be sure to clean the sponge frequently, and then go on to the next wall. About 10 to 15 minutes after the last cleaning, a cement haze will form on the tiles. Clean this off with a clean white rag or cheesecloth. Be careful not to disturb the grout lines.

Once the grout has hardened for 24 hours, vacuum the dust and grit from the floor around the tub or shower pan. After 72 hours, apply a coat of liquid silicone sealer to grout joints; wait 24 hours and apply a second coat. Caulk may be applied at this time; its application is described in Chapter Ten.

PRO TIP

Conceal screws in the wall jambs of your shower door with matching colored plastic screw caps available at your local home center.

IN DETAIL

There are two types of shower rods: compression and screw-in. When installing a compression-type rod on tile, do not overtighten it—the pressure can crack the tiles. Depending on the thickness of your fiberglass tub/shower surround, it might be necessary to install the rod above the panels to protect the panels from denting and/or cracking. To install a screw-in shower rod in tile, use a ceramic or masonry drill bit and drill slowly so you don't crack the tile. Avoid drilling holes through grout lines, which are tough to seal. (It's also easy to crack tile at the grout line.) Always drill and insert fasteners through the solid surface of the tile. You may want to install the rod above the tile or fiberglass surround—hopefully backer boards were installed in the framing stage to properly support the rod.

The unusual design of Senza's door track (by Kohler) keeps the bypassing doors evenly apart mechanically but allows water to roll off the low end of the track and back into the tub. Plastic clean-outs at each end of the track allow water to drain from the channels each time a door opens.

Finishing Touch: A Shower Door

Once the tile, grout, and caulk are completely cured, it's time to install the tub/shower door. Choose a door with the least amount of maintenance—if possible, a trackless door or one with an L-track—but make sure it's in keeping with your bath's style.

The biggest problem with tub/shower doors is leakage around the track if it's not properly sealed. Also, the track needs regular and thorough cleaning—especially a single or double U-shaped track designed for bypassing doors. There are tub/shower doors with no track—the panels of the shower door tip in at the bottom toward the tub to deflect water back into the tub and to help keep water off the sill of the tub. Shower doors are also available in a bifold style. These bifold doors are also manufactured for shower stalls and are a sensible choice in bathrooms where space is at a premium.

Glass companies also make and install custom tub/shower doors—an option worth considering, especially if you have an unusual shower design. In our bathroom we chose the Senza bypass shower door by Kohler for its unusual track design, referred to as a curb.

Shower door step-by-step

When installing a tub/shower door, be sure to follow the instructions that come with the unit. The door is a finish piece, so be patient and carefully work through the directions step-by-step. Before beginning, be sure to protect the tub and the floor in front of it.

The success of this shower door project will be based on the installation of your sidewall jambs. Make sure they go in level. Recheck the wall jambs for plumb and mark the holes with a pencil in preparation for drilling. Manufacturers usually supply wall anchors, but if backer boards are in place, you can eliminate wall anchors and use

Hold the wall jambs in place temporarily with painters' blue masking tape and recheck your jamb positions with a level.

stainless steel wood screws long enough to penetrate the framing members behind the wallboard if the manufacturer's supplied screws aren't long enough.

When drilling into the tile, be sure that the masonry bit has a sharp tip. Proceed slowly, applying very little pressure to prevent cracking the tile. If the door is being installed in an existing bathroom and you are not sure if there is any backing, take your time. Drill through the tile with a ceramic drill bit and stop just when the bit is through the tile. Finish up with a small wood bit—you will be able to feel if the drill is biting into wood. If no wood is evident, continue with the ceramic bit and insert plastic anchors.

As you install the side jambs, start with the center screws and work outward; tighten the first screw in each jamb just enough to hold the jamb in place. Follow with the remaining screws and tighten enough to securely hold each jamb. Take care not to overtighten the screws if you are working on a tile wall.

The header will be a tight fit. Its width is shorter than the enclosure by just the width of a hacksaw blade. Because the header's width might be about the same width of your room, watch those walls as you position it.

Our track sits on the tub's curb and is held in place with the aid of the clean-out, the screws passing through it into each wall jamb, and the caulk/sealant applied to the manufacturer's recommendations. Your actual installation may be different.

Once the necessary accessory items have been added to your doors, it's time to hang them in the header's track. In my case, the doors are designed to be higher than the track on the tub's curb. I installed the inside door first, followed by the outside door. After the doors were in position, I snapped the plastic guide connectors into the track and slid them into the bottom channel of each door. Once the

end caps were installed, the doors were securely locked in the track. Your installation is likely to be different. Check both doors to make sure they slide across the tracks freely and that no further adjustments are required.

Finally, follow the manufacturer's directions for caulking the tub/shower surround and shower door, and let the caulk cure for at least 72 hours before using. For detailed information on finishing up with caulk, see Chapter Ten.

It's hard to wait 72 hours before using your tub or shower, but put that time to good use by installing moldings and other finish trim as described in the next chapter.

The wall jamb is installed, but the final screws won't be put in until the track is ready for installation. Tighten these screws by hand, not with a power tool.

After the hanger bracket and towel bars are in place on both doors, they are ready to lift into position.

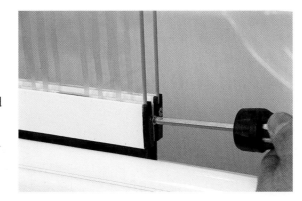

Once the plastic guide connectors were in place, I fastened the end caps, inside door first, using the screws provided.

CHAPTER EIGHT
Moldings

You've reached a point in remodeling where the walls are painted or wallpaper is hung, and the cabinet, countertop, and tiles are set. The flooring is finished and the shower enclosure is in place. The next step is to set the door. Then you'll be ready to install the finish trim around the door, the window, the ceiling, and the floor.

Setting the door is the starting point for trim installation. It's important to correctly set the door to ensure that it is fully functional. A properly hung door will also help you to achieve correct hardware placement and accurate miter cuts for the door casing.

This chapter walks you through these installations and shares tips finish carpenters use for a professional look. Attention to details is important as this finish work is highly visible. Carefully review and follow the guidelines and photos in this chapter.

IN DETAIL

If you're going to install a prehung door, you'll need pine or
cedar shims and finish nails:
2½ in. (8d) for installing jambs
and 1¼ in. (3d) for doorstops;
casings will require 1¼ in. (3d)
for the nose and 1¾ in. (5d) for
the butt. Depending on wall
thickness, you might need 2-in.
(6d) nails instead of 1¾ in. A
7-in. double-edge pull-to-cut saw
will come in handy to trim off
the shims.

These shims are correctly placed.

**Use shims to
achieve a uniform
gap between the
top of the door
and the bottom
side of the frame.**

Hanging and Trimming a Door

My bathroom plans involved relocating
the door. I decided that it was easier to
remove the wall completely and frame a new
one—with a plumb rough door opening that
would accept a new prehung door. Your remodeling project may be less involved, but if you are
setting a new prehung door, use the following
guidelines.

I recommend that you start with a prehung
door assembly that includes the door hung on its
frame, the hinges and doorstops, and prebored
holes for the handle and strike. (Installing a door
blank is more labor- and time-consuming.)
Before purchasing an assembly, decide which way
the door will swing.

A bathroom door should normally swing into
the room and up against a wall, not out into a
hallway. You don't want the door to swing in and
hit the toilet, vanity cabinet, or towel bar. Where
space is at a real premium, the layout might call
for a pocket door, which slides back into the wall.
This type of door requires an opening to accommodate both the door and its pocket.

The floor covering in your bathroom can also
affect how you install the door. If your door

swings into the bathroom over vinyl flooring, you might want to cut off a portion of the bottom of the jambs and drop the entire unit closer to the floor covering. Just make sure that it clears the floor for its entire swing. Some door manufacturers provide up to 1½ in. of space from the bottom of the door to the bottom of the jambs, which will leave a ¼-in. to ½-in. clearance above a throw rug or carpeting and pad. If you're using ceramic floor tile, be sure to measure carefully to ensure that the door clears the tile. Remember that a ½-in. gap will be required between the bottom of the door and the finish floor for proper ventilation. If you leave less of a gap, you'll need to keep the door ajar when showering.

Hanging a door

Before beginning, make sure that the floor between the jambs is level. If the floor is uneven, don't install the door to follow the floor; the door won't operate properly. If the floor slopes from one side of the frame to the other, cut the bottom of one of the jambs to drop the top of the doorframe so that the gap above the door will be even. The trick is to check the gap on the hinge side of the door at the top of the frame and adjust the jamb on the bore (handle) side of the door to that measurement.

If your door has removable doorstops, take them off—but leave the stop in place on the top of the frame. This stop will be removed later, but for now it helps to keep the door from swinging freely and possibly damaging the hinge side of the door.

I find it easier to install a door and place shims if I work from the doorstop side, i.e., the front of the door when closed (not the backside that opens against the wall). With that in mind, place the door in the rough opening. Insert shims from both sides of the door opening between the backsides of the jambs and the framing of the rough

A removable doorstop is held next to a one-piece doorframe with built-in doorstops. With built-in doorstops, position your nails on both sides of it and, if necessary, directly into its center.

opening at the top corners, then insert them at the bottom near the floor. Finally put them in place near the handle and hinges (shims can be positioned either above or below the strike area). The resulting gap should be uniform. If it's not, either push shims in or pull them out to close or open the gap. Because the shims are tapered, you can gradually and accurately adjust the gap.

Next, nail the frame into the rough opening using 8d finish nails, beginning on the hinge

+ SAFETY FIRST

When cutting a shim with a utility knife, don't try to get enough leverage to cut through it all at once by placing your free hand on the jamb just under the shim. It's too easy to slash yourself when the knife's razor blade comes off the shim. Instead, score the back of the shim with many light cuts.

PRO **TIP**

Have a helper hold the door flush with the front edge of the jamb while you install the bore-side stop against the door's front.

TRADE SECRET

If you find after installing your door that it does not close properly up against the bore-side doorstop, most likely your walls are not plumb. Even if your walls are finished you may still be able to remedy the situation by nudging the wall in or out at the bottom plate on either side of the door. The simplest way to move the wall is to lay a 2×6 flat up against the wall near the door to span at least three framing members. Place a 2×4 or 2×6 the same length flat on the floor against the first and, holding it with one foot, smack the edge into the wall with a sledgehammer. After moving the wall, secure it by angling one or more 3-in. screws through the wallboard, through the side of the bottom plate and into the subfloor.

Using Shims Correctly

Remember that shims are tapered. If two shims are placed on top of each other, thin end to butt end, you will get a uniformly sized piece of wood (A). Sliding one past the other allows you to control the thickness and make adjustments to the gap between the face of the frame and the door's edge (B). You must install the shims as shown in A or B. Installing the shims as shown in (C) will cause the door to bind on one side (cant) and prevent it from closing properly.

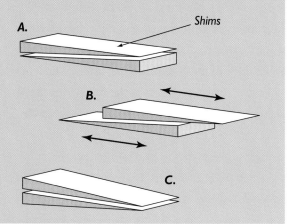

Proper Usage of Shims
A and B show correct use of shims; C is incorrect.

A.   Shims

B.

C.

A pneumatic nailer is much faster and easier to use than a hammer when setting the door frame.

Make sure that your utility knife has a sharp blade. Dull blades have a tendency to split the shims.

126

side. Use two nails and spread them as far apart as possible without getting too close to the trimmer edges. Make sure the finish nails pass through the shims and are long enough to pierce the framing member to hold the doorframe stable. Nail into the faces of the jambs, through the shims, and into the trimmers. It is not necessary to put nails in the top of the doorframe. Set the nails using a nail set, and cut the shims off by scoring them on the wall side with a utility knife and breaking them off with your hand. You might need to score the shim more than once. Be careful not to cut the side of the jamb with your utility knife if you have to cut from the door side.

Once the door is in position, remove the top doorstop, and then install the doorstop on the

Depending on the wood used for the jamb, you may have to predrill nail holes to prevent splits. To set the nail, use a nail set that is the same diameter as the finish nail.

Trimming a Door

To trim a door using a circular saw, lay the door across two sawhorses (covered with cardboard or carpet). Apply masking tape to your planned cutting line; measure and mark that line on top of the tape. Score the line using a straightedge and a utility knife. If you're not using a jig with a base, as shown in the photo, apply 12-in. masking paper where the circular saw will ride as you make the cut. Use a clamped straightedge to guide the base of the saw, and cut 1/16 in. on the "waste" side of your scored line.

The score mark prevents the door from splintering as you cut, but you must take care not to put too much pressure up against the straightedge causing the saw to cut into the score mark. After the cut, peel off the masking tape toward the cut line (peeling in the other direction may lift the veneer if it's a hollow-core door). Use a hand block sander to knock

down both sides of the cut edge to the score mark and create a slight bevel. This bevel prevents the veneer from ripping or peeling if something gets caught underneath the door as it opens or closes.

Use a saw guide (instead of masking tape, masking paper, and a straightedge) to protect the door's surface from the shoe of the circular saw and to help direct the saw during the cut.

IN DETAIL

This photo shows an attractive 1/4-in. reveal where the casing meets the door jamb. The side casings are temporarily installed while the top casing piece is being trial fitted, an important step before final nailing. If the miter joint fits correctly but the casing piece doesn't lie flat against the wall, place a cardboard shim behind the molding near the miter to keep the casing in plane while you nail it.

bore side of the door. On the hinge side, it's important not to position the doorstop directly up against the door. Keep the hinge doorstop back from the face of the door at least 1/16 in. so that the door will clear it. (Slightly adjust that measurement to account for clearance once the door has been painted or finished.) Use 3d finish nails to attach the doorstop on the hinge side, and set the nails. Finally, reinstall the top doorstop with a 3d nail at each end and one in the center. To check your installation, close the door. The bore side of the door should touch the full length of the doorstop. The top doorstop from the bore side should gradually pull out from the face of the door as it nears the hinge side doorstop with its 1/16-in. gap.

Door casings

Before installing door casing (molding), check the wall near the doorframe. If the wallboard is raised slightly above the face of the frame, use a hammer to pound in the wallboard close to the frame. This will allow the nose (normally the

Jamb Extension
Treat the exposed jamb extension like a normal doorframe.

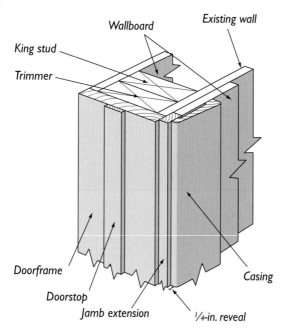

thin side) of the casing to lie flat on the frame's edge.

If the wall extends out farther than the frame, a situation that occurs frequently when new wallboard is applied over existing walls, attach wooden strips (referred to as "jamb extensions") to the edges of the frame flush to the wall. Hold back the extension about 1/4 in. from the edge of the frame, and then hold the casing back about 1/4 in. from the edge of the extension. If the doorframe installation doesn't require extensions, then hold the casing back 1/4 in. to create a reveal on the edge of the frame.

Installing casing

I find it easiest to install the casing by starting with the side jambs. First, measure the casing by standing it up against the jamb and marking it at the bottom edge of the top frame. Add an extra 1/4 in. for the top reveal, and cut the casing using an electric miter saw, or hand saw in a miter box, at 45°.

Temporarily nail the two mitered side casings in place using 3d nails through the nose—the portion of the casing nearest the door opening—and 5d or 6d into the butt (the thick outer part) of the casing. Next, size the top casing by measuring from outside edge to outside edge of the side jamb casings. It's a good idea to add 1/16 in. in case the frame is out of square. Then cut the top casing, with a 45° degree angle in at each edge, and fit it into place between the two side jamb casings. If the doorframe has been set in properly, as earlier described, then casings cut at 45° angles should fit.

When you are satisfied with the fit of the joints, complete the nailing and set the nails. If the casings are prefinished, use a matching putty stick to camouflage the nail holes and wipe off any excess putty with a white rag and some solvent; otherwise, fill the nail holes with a sandable filler that will accept stain or paint.

Moldings

Now it's time to trim out the window and install crown and base moldings—wooden, rubber, or ceramic. I'll start with the window.

Windows

Trimming out a window is similar to casing out a door. However, windows installed into either a 2×4 or 2×6 rough opening will need jambs constructed to extend from the face frame flush with the finish wall (see Frame Extension on p. 130).

The place where the window is located in your bathroom—whether it's in the tub/shower area or farther away from direct contact with water—will determine the type of material used to construct the extension. In Chapter Seven I explained how to wrap a window above the tub with either tile or a Swanstone® window-trim kit. In this section I discuss a window with frame extensions constructed from wood, a suitable choice when moisture is not an issue.

Trimming a window. Before making the extensions, begin by checking to see that the window sits level in the rough opening. If the window has been installed closer to one trimmer than to the other, or closer to the header than to the sill, attach furring strips to the framing material of the rough opening to create a uniform measurement around the outer edge of the frame

Drive nails partially until you trial fit the next piece of casing.

With the side casings temporarily in place, measure for your top piece.

Secure the corner at the top of the glued miter with a nail coming in from the top of the casing. Protect the wall surface with a piece of cardboard as you hammer.

TRADE SECRET

Perfect crown molding corner joints are difficult because a combination of miter and bevel cuts is required. Most electric miter saw manufacturers include a table of degree cuts in their manuals, and many include this data on the saws. Common settings include:

- 38° miter at 31.61°, bevel at 33.86°
- 40° miter at 32.73°, bevel at 32.82°
- 45° miter at 35.26°, bevel at 30.01°

Placing the molding finish side down on the miter table may help you achieve accurate miter cuts, but place the molding with its back on the table so you can see the design details. First make cuts according to your calculations and then trial fit. Nail one piece in place and have a helper hold the matching piece while you cut down the joint with a small double-edged pull-to-cut saw. Cutting only the touching areas yields a clean and perfectly fitting joint. When you are satisfied with the fit, use the template to trial fit the remaining corners.

Window Stools and Aprons

Perhaps you remember the plants lined up on your grandma's windowsill and the great detail trim that surrounded that window. You can recreate that look in your own home by extending the window stool out about 1½ in. from the finish wall and lengthening the stool beyond both sides of the window. Some people refer to the stool as the sill, but the interior flat ledge is actually the stool; the sill is the exterior ledge set on a slight angle to shed water. The extensions of the stool beyond the window are called ears. This area provides a platform for the casings. These ears can extend up to 1 in. beyond the wallboard jamb extensions, to just beyond the casings, or they can remain even with the outside edges of the casings. If you choose to install a stool, add an apron under the stool to finish it off.

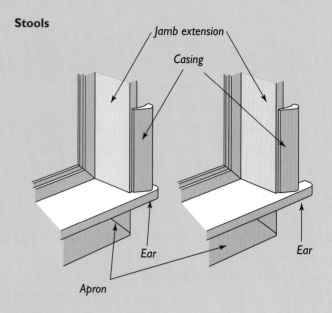

Stools

Aprons

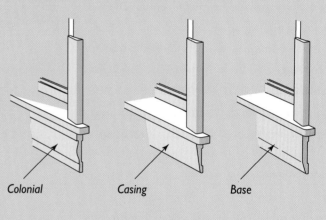

Colonial   Casing   Base

Frame Extension

It's a lot easier to install a completed unit than individual pieces.

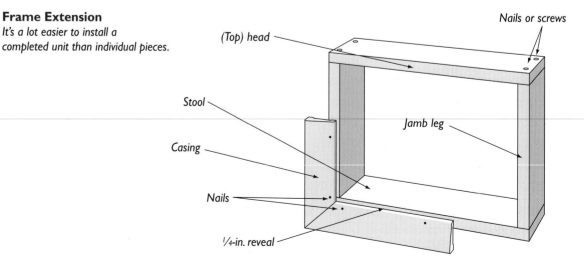

of the window. When the frame extensions are ready to install, they will appear balanced evenly around the face of the window.

Install the top (head) and bottom (sill) extensions first, and then the jamb legs. I prefer to assemble the pieces like a box and then install the box in the rough opening. I always do a trial fit, though. Build in some tolerances to allow for framing irregularities and so the box will not be too large for the rough opening.

Crown molding

There are different styles, designs, shapes, types, and grades of crown molding—from softwood to hardwood to MDF to polyurethane foam, primed or unfinished. Some are constructed of solid material, suitable for staining, while others, like fingerjointed softwoods, are perfect for painting. Because of the high moisture content normally found in a bath, I selected polyurethane foam for my molding material.

Most crown moldings are designed with a crown angle of 45°/45° or 52°/38°. These angle degrees dictate the degree of cuts for the miter, which requires a correct combination of miter and bevel angles. Depending on the type and size of crown molding, you may need an electric miter saw, compound miter saw, or slide compound miter saw to make these cuts. Consider renting one if you don't own one.

Installing crown molding. Mastering the joints of crown molding will dictate the success of its installation. However, the type of molding you select can also make this task easier or more difficult to do. Pine and polyurethane foam are lightweight and easier to work with and install than hardwood moldings. In either case, a second pair of hands and patience will be required to achieve an almost invisible joint.

Preparation. When purchasing molding, select the longest stock available to eliminate joints

This 90° cornice with an egg and dart design by Fypon is easier to install than crown molding as it requires only a miter cut instead of a compound miter cut.

Because urethane molding expands and contracts, I recommend that you add ¼ in. to every 10 ft. and spring the longer moldings into place.

(probably not an issue in an average-sized bath). Now check to see if the room is square; hold a framing square into all the walls' corners. If the room is out of square, you'll have to adjust your miter cuts so the installed molding will appear to be applied squarely in the room. Also check for flat surfaces in the molding installation areas. You may have to float the walls with some drywall mud in areas where the molding doesn't hit the wall.

PRO TIP

When installing wooden crown molding, prevent splitting by drilling pilot holes at the ends of each piece.

IN DETAIL

If more than one piece of molding is needed to run the length of a wall, splice pieces together using a scarf joint centered over a stud. You can cut a scarf joint with your miter saw set at 45°. Cut joining pieces so that their angled cuts overlap.

IN DETAIL

To achieve the maximum illusion of height, paint the ceiling an off-white or cream color, the crown moldings white, and the walls tan or another color. To really make the molding stand out, try painting the small reveal on the bottom edge of the molding to match the wall. It's much easier to paint the reveal and molding as one unit, but this little trick gives depth to the walls and adds extra character to the molding.

For an exact fit, hold the matching piece and insert a double-edge pull-to-cut saw to cut away those areas that are touching.

Cutting the first length: inside corners. Mitered joints are created when two angles come together in the corner, and they're typically cut with an electric miter saw (commonly called a chopsaw) for the best possible cut. However, if the molding you selected has a highly detailed profile, then it's important before you make that first cut to balance the molding's design within its installation space. The goal is to get the two angle pieces to come together so their designs match perfectly in

A pneumatic finish nailer speeds up the installation of crown molding because it countersinks the T-nails.

the corners. This is sometimes hard to achieve, but the extra effort required will produce excellent joints once the molding is completely finished.

Always install on the shortest wall first and add an extra ¼ in. to the length of the long wall moldings so you can spring them into place for a snug fit. It's a good idea to cut a sample piece and temporarily nail it in place in order to fit the permanent piece. This allows you to see that the miters are cut correctly, the pieces meet with no gaps, and their designs match for aesthetic reasons. For the long wall, I suggest that you temporarily tack the center and both ends to wall studs and ceiling joists using 6d to 8d finish nails to make sure you are satisfied with the joints.

It's very helpful to know before nailing crown molding up and into place where those wall studs and ceiling joists are. However, when you know your nails will not make direct contact with solid material (common with lath-and-plaster walls), it's important to shoot every other nail at an angle in the opposite direction to lock the molding into place while the adhesive on the backside cures.

Because I used polyurethane crown moldings, urethane adhesive was required for installation. During our project I used a pneumatic finish nailer with 1¾-in. 18-gauge brad nails (T-nails). If you are not using a pneumatic nailer, use finish

nails to secure the molding—this is where a second pair of hands will be useful. Both adhesive and nails (installed either pneumatically or manually) are necessary for a good installation.

An outside corner. If you're installing crown molding around an outside corner, again use a compound miter saw to make the required cuts. You'll find it easier to work if you place the molding with its back flat on the miter saw's turntable with the ceiling side up against the fence. (A correctly cut outside corner will not show an exposed profile, while an inside corner will.)

Finishing touches. Detail work can make or break the overall appearance of your crown molding, so expect to put some time into it. Once the molding is securely fastened, it's important to fill all nail holes, corners, and edges where the molding meets the ceiling and walls with latex caulk if needed. If you leave some voids—or if the caulk shrinks as it dries—you might have to make a second application of caulk the following day. Finally, prime and apply two coats of paint to the entire molding.

Base molding

The type of floor covering you select will influence your choice of base molding—but your choice should also take into account the style of the room.

Wooden. Wooden base molding can give a bathroom a rich look. Paint or stain the molding before installation. Apply matching stain to your freshly cut miter joints. It also helps to nail the molding to solid backing, such as studs. After you have set the nails, apply a matching putty stick to conceal the nail holes in the stained molding. Excess putty can be removed with a white rag and a solvent that will not hurt the clear finish—use mineral spirits or paint thinner. Read the solvent label to make sure it is safe for use over clear finishes. If your moldings are painted, fill

Add prepainted quarter-round shoe molding to cover the gap between the tile and the base molding. The small mitered return at the end of the molding run was glued in place before the shoe was installed.

the holes with a paintable latex caulk. If you need to use more than one length of molding along a wall, join lengths together with overlapping scarf joints, which are less noticeable than butt joints.

Rubber. Installing rubber base molding, also known as cove base, is not as easy as it looks. First position the piece and mark on the backside, with a pencil, where it will bend around the outside corner. Then bend the base backward and use a utility knife to cut a notch into the back of it at

✚ SAFETY FIRST

Cut rubber base moldings using a utility knife with a sharp razor blade, but take care to prevent injury to yourself or damage to your new floor covering. First, watch your fingers. If you are cutting the molding at floor level, have a plywood board underneath it. Make sure the board is large enough so that when you come off the cut, the blade stays on the board and doesn't hit the floor.

IN DETAIL

When installing cove base molding up against tile, cut it so the shoe of the molding matches the radius of the bull-nose tile. It's a little tricky, but with patience it can be done. I suggest making trial cuts on a scrap piece first before tackling the finished piece. The same applies to cove base butting up against solid-surface apron strips.

TRADE SECRET

If you want to use your existing wooden base molding because it cannot be reproduced—and it's salvageable—then by all means use it. As you remove the molding, label each piece on the backside so you can reinstall it in the same position. I recommend that you repaint or refinish the molding before installation.

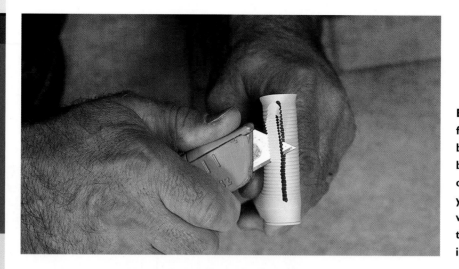

Be extremely careful when cutting the back of the cove base to fit around an outside corner. If you cut too much, it will appear thin at the corner after installation.

To install rubber base around a corner and under a cabinet toekick, install the panel side first and then pull the base around the corner.

the place you marked. Be careful not to cut too much out. Apply a 2-in.-long patch of contact cement (corner installations only) to the wall or cabinet on both sides of the corner and spread contact cement on the corresponding area on the back of the cove base. Follow the manufacturer's instructions and allow sufficient time for the contact cement to dry.

Once the contact cement has dried, spread cove adhesive lengthwise on the remaining section of the piece about 3/8 in. down from the top edge and 1/4 in. from the ends to prevent any adhesive from oozing out. Mount the cove by pushing down on it at the same time you apply it to one side of the wall or cabinet corner. Use your other hand to stabilize the molding so it

doesn't flop onto the finished floor as you work it around the corner.

Most likely you will be using 4-ft. pieces of cove base. When fitting in an area longer than 4 ft., be sure to cut the second piece up to 1/8 in. longer than the measurement of the remaining wall in order to create a snug fit. Temperature changes can cause the base to shrink and open joints.

Inside corners are simple. Begin by gluing your first piece straight into the corner. Then make a 45° angle cut on the cove's shoe of the second piece. Finally, on the backside of that 45° angle, cut away the cove material so the piece will sit properly on the shoe and butt into the adjacent piece. Install the molding on shorter walls first—

the corner walls behind a door, for example—and always install the shortest molding first. Experiment with a scrap piece to get a feel for cutting the material.

Ceramic. I'm a firm believer that a tile floor should have a tile base molding. Start with a trial layout of all your tile before installing it. Next, draw a pencil line ¼ in. lower than the height you want your tile molding to reach. Spread the adhesive up to the pencil mark, then seat the tile. For inside or outside corners, just overlap at an outside corner and butt on an inside corner; be sure to leave the proper grout gap at both intersections. Once done, grout and polish the tiles to complete this phase of the work.

If you're gluing base tiles to a cabinet, scuff the cabinet's finish surface with sandpaper in the area where the tiles will be installed; this creates a better bond for the mastic. Take care not to disturb the finish beyond the tile line.

Now that the door, window, ceiling, and base moldings are installed, you can move on to the next step: installing the electrical and plumbing fixtures and trim.

Determine which side of the molding you are comfortable with when cutting the shoe's 45° angle.

To achieve a tighter inside corner joint, position the molding, scribe it, and cut the scribe. You'll actually cut a small arch at the top, as seen on the left-hand piece, with the shoe cut at a 45° angle.

Remove wallpaper in three quarters of the area over which the ceramic base tile will be installed. If you don't, the mastic will loosen the wallpaper and the tile will pop off.

Finishing Up with

Fixtures

One of the most pleasant parts of remodeling a bathroom is putting in the electrical and plumbing fixtures; installing each piece brings you one step closer to a fully functional bathroom.

It's important, however, to take your time. Work slowly and carefully as you handle each fixture. Every finish piece will be visible, so work to avoid doing damage. Also, make sure to protect the walls and ceiling as you install receptacles, switches, and light fixtures. The vanity countertop, cabinet, shower enclosure, and walls are also vulnerable as you work with both fixtures and tools. This is not the time to rush the project along.

Before you begin, thoroughly read the instructions supplied by the manufacturer. These instructions list the specific tools and materials required for each job. It helps to have them at hand as you work. The professional end result will be worth the time you invest.

IN DETAIL

Before installing a receptacle or switch in its electrical box, remove any wallboard compound in or around the box—including any compound from the screw compartments. A wooden-handled cotton swab is great for this. If wallpaper is involved, remove the wallpaper around the box as well. Take care when using your utility knife, especially if there are live wires in the box.

TRADE SECRET

I find that push-in receptacles (quick connections) are the easiest and the fastest way to go in the final installation of GFCI receptacles and other receptacles or switches. As you purchase receptacles, check to see if you can make quick connections or wrap the wire around a screw, or even do both, when connecting wires to the terminals.

Electrical Fixtures

When I'm finishing up an electrical installation in a bathroom, I like to work in this order: wall plates for the receptacles and switches, light fixtures next, and then the grills for exhaust fans and heat lamps. Assuming your GFCI and other receptacles and switches are already in place (Chapter Four), you, too, are ready to begin.

Wall plates

You can have wall plates made to match your decorating scheme, or you can purchase unfinished wooden ones, as we did, and stain them to match the cabinetry and wooden toilet seat. You can also cover plastic wall plates with wallpaper.

Light fixtures

When you're hanging a light fixture, make sure that the side of the crossbar marked "GND" faces out, that mounting screws don't interfere with outlet-box screw holes, and that the crossbar, securely fastened, sits squarely in the outlet box. Adjust the threaded nipple in the crossbar so it protrudes just enough through the base to accommodate a finial (nut). Some manufacturers supply

These wooden switch and receptacle wall plates were stained and finished to match the room's décor.

Be careful to not overtighten the finial—it doesn't take much to crack the glass.

A little paint and proper spacing make the diffuser and grill barely noticeable.

a washer and extra nut to secure the back of the base and provide support for the finial.

Place a clean white towel between the base and wall to protect them while you put on the wire nuts (both black and white) and attach a crimp connector to the grounding wires. Wire nuts can support the weight of most sidelights and flush-mount fixtures, but you'll need a second pair of hands when installing other types of fixtures. Make sure the wires are tucked inside the outbox before installing the base. Also check to see that no wires get caught under the base as you secure it. Take care as you use a wrench to tighten the finial close to the base to avoid any damage to the surface. Finally, set the glass.

Diffusers and grills

Diffusers and grills are the finish plastic trims mounted to heat lamps and vent fixtures. By themselves they can be unattractive, but new spray paints on the market that bond to plastics can make them blend in with the ceiling. Whether or not you paint them, they are still necessary to trim out the unit.

My Deflect-o fan uses a small round diffuser system that is hardly noticeable in my wallboard ceiling. Rather than using a locking ring, I applied latex caulk to the back of the collar flange and allowed it to set up for 24 hours before setting in the diffuser. The heat lamp grill I used is similar to those found on standard ceiling fans, except that the grill is slotted. Secure the springs or wire hooks to hold the grill in place. Make sure the springs are secure before you let go of the grill.

Recessed Grills

If your ceiling is textured, the grill of your heat lamp may not fit smoothly up against it, and light might shine out from under the grill across the ceiling. To correct this, recess the grill.

First, install the grill and bulb. When you're satisfied with the fit, trace around the perimeter of the grill with a pencil. Remove the grill and score along the pencil line with a utility knife. Using a 1-in. putty knife, remove the texture between the fixture's opening edge and the score mark. Check the fit, and then reinstall the grill. Look for places that need to be recut or scraped. Now remove the grill again and use your finger to apply wet wallboard compound around the inside cut of the recessed area to make it blend into the rest of the ceiling. This will create an inside corner and round off the edge of the cut. When it's dry, prime and paint.

After priming and painting, the recessed area cut for the grill blends in perfectly with the ceiling.

PRO TIP

If you can't place the flange for the shut-off valve over the pipe, turn the flange around and work it partway over the pipe to stretch the prongs.

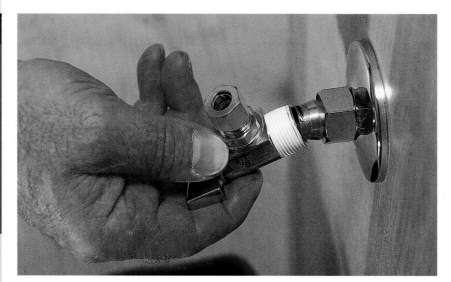

Remember to wind Teflon tape clockwise as you apply it; work in the same direction that the nut will screw on to the threads (the "rightie-tightie" rule).

TRADE SECRET

Completely clean supply lines before installing vanity and shutoff valves. Remove all wallboard compound and paint that may be on them. The pipes are easier to clean when you have full access to them, and it will help to guarantee that no water leaks after shutoff valves are installed. It also provides a smooth, clean surface for the tubing cutter. Measure accurately and drill the back of the cabinet to accept the supply lines and drain.

Washbasins

Before setting the washbasin, install the shutoff valves and the main drain because it's easier to lean over into the cabinet than to do these installations on your back. Then assemble the faucet and the drain/stopper fitting and mount them on the sink.

Shutoff valves

If your older home has galvanized pipes, install threaded shutoff valves. Before you begin, be sure to clean any debris or foreign material, such as wallboard compound, adhesive, or paint, from the supply lines—galvanized or copper—that extend from the wall or floor. For copper, mark the pipe

Flexible Hose Connectors

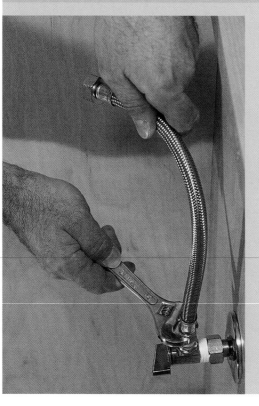

With the shutoff valves installed, take time to tighten the screws that secure the handles. Then remove the 3/8-in. compression nut and ring and look down into the supply outlet to see if the valve is in the shutoff position. If it's not, put it into the shutoff position, and then turn the water on to check the valve for leaks. If it's going to leak, water will show around the compression nut on the copper pipe. Just tighten the nut until the leak stops. Now attach the flexible hose connectors to the shutoff valves. Purchase hose connectors with stainless steel braided jackets and 3/8-in. female compression thread for the shutoff valve on one side, and 1/2-in. female pipe thread to connect to the threads of the faucet on the other.

Attach the flexible hose connector to the 3/8-in. threads using an open-end adjustable wrench.

about 2 in. from the wall. Close the main shutoff valve and drain the system. Put a bucket under the supply line, and position a midget tubing cutter just outside the mark (to give a little extra pipe length). Water will leak just as the pipe starts to break. Let it completely drain before finishing the cut. Now slide the flanges over the pipe, convex side out, and up against the back of the cabinet.

To install the compression valve, slide the compression nut (and compression ring) onto the pipe. Leave some space between the flange and the back of the nut. Spread pipe joint compound with Teflon® (or use Teflon tape) on the threads before you slide the shutoff valve over the pipe. Apply constant pressure to the valve as you slide the ring and nut up to the threads on the valve, and then tighten the nut manually. Position a wrench on the shutoff valve and use another wrench to tighten the nut. Take care not to mar the face of the flange with the wrench.

Drain and P-trap

A standard washbasin drain with pop-up assembly has a 1¼-in. tailpiece. P-traps and trap adapters are available in 1¼ in. and 1½ in., but the 1¼-in. P-trap is more readily available. A 1½-in. P-trap

will require a reducing slip-joint washer (1¼ in. to 1½ in.) at the washbasin tailpiece. If you purchased a 1¼-in. P-trap, then locate the reducing slip-joint washer at the trap arm. From here on I will assume a 1½-in. P-trap. The drainpipe is

Washbasin Drain Extensions

The tailpieces that come with washbasin faucets are normally too short to reach higher vanity cabinets unless the drain is raised during the rough-in. In cases like this there are two options: one is to remove the tailpiece and thread in an extended tailpiece, which eliminates using a 6-in. drain extension, and the other is to install a drain extension. However, a 12-in. (extended) tailpiece needs to be cut down to make the entire assembly fit.

Because the cabinet was higher, a 6-in. ABS drain extension was added to make the connection to the tailpiece.

Before you apply cement, cover the bottom of the cabinet to protect it from drips.

IN DETAIL

It's easy to miscalculate where to drill your supply line and main drain holes in the back of a vanity cabinet. Escutcheons (finish flanges) can cover any supply line "miscalculations," providing the mistake is within the flange circumference. If you drill the drainpipe hole too large, hide the gap with a split floor and ceiling plate, available in different sizes. Pull it apart, fit it around the drainpipe behind the trap adapter, and lock it together.

Undermount Application

No mechanical fasteners support the undermount washbasin in this custom countertop application.

Finish countertop

Caulk

Undermount washbasin

Plywood

Reinforcement

Use a latex caulk with an adhesive base and apply a healthy bead to the underside of the washbasin rim so it will ooze out around the perimeter of the washbasin.

Having the faucet already in place provides a solid handle while setting the Swanstone® washbasin into the vanity countertop.

usually stubbed out through the wall, but I find it easier to put in the vanity cabinet if it isn't. (It is also easier to work on the stubout if the countertop or washbasin has not yet been installed; that eliminates working in such a tight space.) Apply the appropriate solvent cement to the inside of the 90° drain elbow to accept the drain stubout. Next, cut the drain stubout to accept the trap adapter, and then glue the trap adapter.

Slide the trap arm into the trap adapter and loosely tighten the slip nut. Slide a slip nut and reducing washer over the tailpiece. Simultaneously slip the trap bend up and over the tailpiece and up to the trap arm. Loosely tighten the trap arm slip nut and slide the reducing washer and slip nut down to the trap bend. Support the trap bend with one hand and tighten the slip nut for a watertight fit. Tighten the remaining slip joints to secure the system and check for leaks.

Basic sink installations

There are four basic types of sink installations: undermount, drop-in, wall-hung, and preformed vanity top and bowl.

Undermount. Washbasins mounted directly to the countertop's underside or recessed into a substrate need support under the basin's rim. In the first case, apply latex caulk to the top of the sink rim. In the second, apply caulk to the recessed area and to the top of the sink's rim, holding it back by ½ in. in both situations. Finish caulking will be discussed in Chapter Ten.

Drop-in. These sinks require a cutout in order to be mounted in the countertop. I prefer to make washbasin cutouts in unfinished substrate rather than in the finish countertop. If your cutout hasn't been made yet, use the template supplied with the washbasin. First trace the template, and then drill a hole larger than a jigsaw blade just inside the traced line. Finally, use a jigsaw to cut the hole.

Before you cut, mask the bottom side of the jigsaw shoe to protect the countertop. Use a blade that's not too coarse and take your time to cut carefully. If you don't have an extra pair of hands when making the cutout, cut the section out in two pieces to prevent damage to the finished laminate top or to the floor of the cabinet if it should fall. For washbasins with hold-down clips, use plumber's putty between the basin and the counter. For a self-rimming basin, apply caulk—it may be supplied by the manufacturer—and drop the basin into place.

Drop-in composite basins without factory-drilled holes have pilot holes on the underside to indicate the 4- or 8-in. faucet spreads. You'll need to drill holes into the washbasin to accept the faucet assembly before you can mount the sink in the countertop. For an undermount situation, put the washbasin in place and drill through the pilot holes up through the countertop. Remove the sink and then cut the actual holes from the finish side of the countertop using a hole-saw. Just line up the center bit with each pilot hole and start drilling. Finally, using the same hole saw, cut the holes in the undermount sink.

Know whether the faucet spread is 4 in. or 8 in. before drilling pilot holes from the underside. Use a hole saw to drill the final holes from the finish side.

PRO TIP

If plumber's putty doesn't completely soften up after working it a few minutes, it may be too old to be usable, and it should be replaced.

IN DETAIL

If you have ever removed an older faucet or put one in after the countertop has been installed, you know that removing or installing basin nuts is a challenge; they are tucked up behind the washbasin in the back of the cabinet, and it's difficult to reach and see them at the same time. The smaller your cabinet is, the harder this job will be.

A plastic nut basin wrench, however, offers a good solution to this problem. It can reach and turn plastic mounting nuts on faucets, sprayers, and ballcocks. The notched ends are designed to self-center on 2-, 3-, 4-, and 6-tab nuts and to fit metal hex nuts. The 11-in. length makes it ideal for tight-clearance pedestal washbasins.

Plumber's Putty

Because plumber's putty contains mineral and vegetable oils, it shouldn't be used on some building materials, such as marble and some plastics. Porous materials will absorb oils from the putty and leave a stain. Contact the manufacturer of the product you plan to use it on to make sure you avoid damaging finish surfaces.

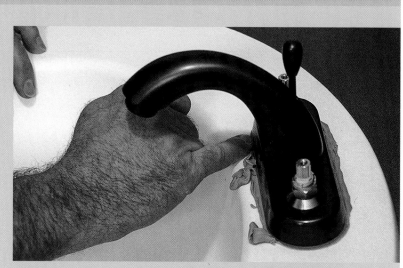

The faucet should sit at room temperature, assembled, for an hour before you make a final pass at tightening the basin nuts.

Wall-hung. This type of washbasin requires mounting a wall bracket about 33 in. off the finish floor or at a height that is comfortable for you. Make sure this bracket is level. Use lag screws and center the bracket over the drainpipe. The lag screws should be fastened to a backer board that was installed during framing rough-in. Mount the washbasin on the bracket and apply latex caulk where the sink meets the wall.

Preformed. This washbasin, a popular item in many bathrooms today, comes molded right into a countertop; you have only a single unit to install. Trial fit the unit in the cabinet first. If it doesn't fit properly, you might have to sand out any imperfections on the backside.

Once you are satisfied with the fit, apply clear silicone caulk to the cabinet frame and corner braces. Apply enough caulk around the perimeter of the cabinet and an ample amount on the corner blocks to ensure a secure bond to the cabinet. Place the counter and basin unit down over the cabinet. Check the overhangs and how it sits up against the wall(s) before you firmly press the unit down into the caulk.

Plumbing Fixtures

With this project, I will start by installing the faucet and end with trimming the bathtub. When installing plumbing fixtures, make sure to follow the manufacturer's instructions. You should always be very careful when handling these finish pieces. Use the proper tools and take care not to mar or scratch the finishes or to overtighten screws on a fixture or trim piece. For threaded items, be sure to use pipe joint compound or wrap white Teflon sealing tape clockwise around the threads to achieve a good seal.

Faucets

If I haven't mentioned it earlier, I find it easier if the faucet is mounted to the washbasin before the basin is set into the countertop. However, if you have the proper tools, the project can go smoothly—even if the washbasin has been installed first. After the faucet you can install the basin drain with pop-up stopper.

Plumber's putty will become your best friend in this stage of the work. Soften it up, apply it to the underside of the plastic bottom plate, and

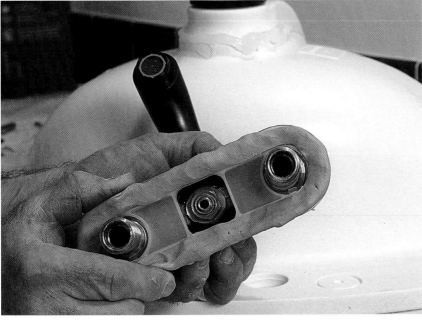

Be sure to fill the perimeter cavity of the plastic bottom plate with plumber's putty.

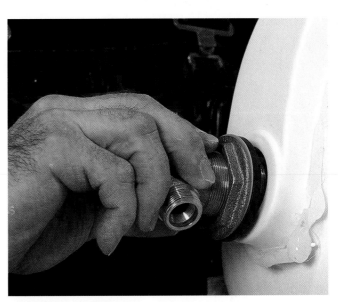

The pop-up body is fastened from the underside of the washbasin to the flange threads.

position the plate over the faucet cutouts. Place the faucet into the center of the holes and hold it while you apply and finger-tighten the large friction washers and basin nuts. Check the position of the faucet before securing the nuts using a plastic nut basin wrench. Be sure to apply Teflon tape for three or four clockwise revolutions to the faucet inlet shanks. Place the lever trim (hub) according to the manufacturer's instructions.

Basin drain with pop-up stopper.
Carefully adjusting the pop-up stopper and rod before you install the washbasin in the countertop will prevent you from having to crawl into the cabinet later. The following steps will guide you in completing the last of the faucet assembly.

Apply plumber's putty to the underside of the drain flange—enough so it oozes out, but not so much that it interferes with the threads on the flange. Push the flange into the center of the washbasin's outlet hole. Hold onto the flange and fasten the pop-up body from the underside of the washbasin to the flange threads. Tighten by hand until the flange starts to twist. Then apply pressure against the flange and tighten the body nut so the rubber washer is snug to the washbasin. Now hold

Install the drain-rod assembly before you drop in the sink.

PRO **TIP**

Showerhead arms have both short and long ends. Mount the showerhead on the shorter end of the arm.

IN DETAIL

Before installing the shower arm, clean out any wallboard compound in the hole and on the threads of the brass 90° drop-ear elbow and check that the hole is not plugged with compound. Then install the long end of the shower arm into the finish (convex) side of the finish flange. Apply Teflon tape clockwise to the threads of the long arm to prevent leakage, and then install it into the elbow. Tighten by hand, then slide the finish flange up against the shower wall.

the upper portion of the pop-up body and tighten the body nut using an adjustable hex or slip-nut wrench. The ball rod opening should face dead center on the pop-up rod hole.

Insert the stopper in the position the manufacturer recommends and install the ball rod assembly. Do not overtighten the nut because it will distort the rod. I apply Teflon tape sparingly on the threads before assembly for a no-leak installation. Use a slip-nut wrench around the body nut to hold everything in place as you tighten the tailpiece. Hand tightening is usually sufficient.

Slide one of the holes in the pop-up rod strap extension over the shaft of the ball rod and secure the clip. One leg of the clip goes on one side of the strap and the other leg goes on the other side. Now secure the pop-up rod to the strap by sliding the rod into the two holes and securing the wing nut. Fine-tune the adjustment by making sure you can easily grasp the rod knob in the down position (stopper up/drain open) and that the rod knob doesn't hit any portion of the faucet. When the rod is pulled, the stopper will lower to close the drain. After the supply lines are hooked up, fill the washbasin to test the stopper for leakage. As a

final step, remove excess plumber's putty from around the drain flange.

Bathtub

Before trimming out the tub/shower area, take time to protect the bathtub with cardboard and/or painting tarps in case a tool or piece of hardware accidentally falls.

Showerhead. Push the shower arm's long side into the convex side of the flange. Wrap Teflon tape around the threads on the long side. Insert it into the supply line elbow and hand tighten.

Tub Spout. For my Price Pfister spout trim piece, I glued two rubber washers (2¾-in. by ⅝-in. center hole) with clear rubber silicone to the center back of the piece and let it cure for 72 hours. Then I filled the space where the copper stub protrudes from the wall with silicone caulk and allowed it to cure for 72 hours.

To prevent water from getting behind the wall, apply siliconized acrylic to the back of the trim piece (if provided) around the outside perimeter and install it over the copper stub. Also, apply latex caulk to the front of the trim just around the copper stub and follow it up with the protective washer if one is supplied with the spout.

Don't forget to wind Teflon tape clockwise on the showerhead arm threads. Take care when using a wrench so you don't mar the showerhead.

Loosely install the tub spout upside down so you can tighten the clamp screw with a hex wrench. Turn the spout to its correct position, apply constant pressure to the piece, and finish securing it.

Shower valve assembly. The shower trim contains pre-installed foam, so there is no need to add caulk to the trim. Make sure the hole in the trim points down so that if any water gets behind the trim, it has an escape route. Also be sure to remove the valve template before installing the trim piece. After the trim has been added, follow it up with the screw retainer sleeve with the washer toward the valve. Tighten by hand. Attach the shower lever using the screws supplied by the manufacturer; follow it up by pushing in the O-ring finish button. The guidelines here apply to the Price Pfister unit I chose for my bathroom; follow the instructions supplied by the manufacturer of your shower valve assembly.

Trip lever and plunger assembly. Our plunger rod has a brass screw clamp that allows the rods to be adjusted. (Yours may differ.) To determine if the plunger is adjusted correctly, flip the trip lever up to close the drain and partially fill the tub. Be prepared to adjust the plunger assem-

Cut the copper stub 2¼ in. out from the face of the trim for the tub spout.

Luxury Showerheads

Now that the shower area is complete, the fun really begins—finding the right showerhead. While remodeling my bathroom I reviewed a few shower heads from Waterpik Technologies, each with different features. Here are three worth considering.

The AquaFall® makes shower spray feel like natural rainfall.

The Cascadia® delivers both full-body and concentrated power sprays.

The Misting Massage® has seven settings—including steam.

PRO TIP

When working on the toilet flange, plug the soil pipe with a rag or newspapers to keep gases from entering and debris from lodging in the pipe.

WHAT CAN GO WRONG

A solid supply tube (left) can be difficult to work with compared to a flexible braided stainless steel supply line (right). If the shutoff valve is not positioned at the correct distance away from the wall and centered under the ballcock tailpiece on the bottom left-hand side of the tank, a tube bending spring will be required to fit the solid supply tube to the application. If the shutoff valve is off-center and too close to the ballcock, the solid tube will be difficult to bend.

Tube bending spring.

After you put the plunger assembly back into the drain/overflow tube, you should find that there's a ¼-in. to ½-in. play in the trip lever between the open and closed drain positions.

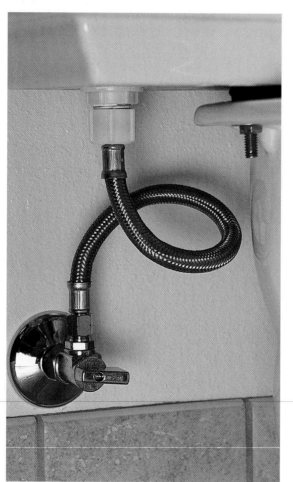

A 9-in. toilet supply line was not available at my home improvement center. I had to settle for a 12-in. line; it's a little long, but it works.

bly a few times. Access the plunger assembly by removing the two screws that attach the cover of the overflow trip lever.

Toilets

There are many components to assemble when you're installing a toilet, just as there are with a sink. Here I will explain how to install the shutoff valve, flange, wax bowl ring, and the toilet itself.

Shutoff valve

I prefer a compression-fitting shutoff valve and a flexible braided stainless steel toilet connector for a supply line from the shutoff valve to the toilet. Start by cutting the copper toilet water-supply pipe from 1¼ in. to 2 in. long with a tubing cutter. Slide the flange on (convex side out), then the nut, and finally the compression ring. Wind Teflon tape clockwise (or apply pipe joint compound with Teflon) on the threads and slide the valve onto the copper stub. Have a clean white towel nearby to keep fitting parts and fingers clean. Tighten the nut to the valve using two wrenches—applying constant pressure against the valve.

If you're using a solid tube for a supply line, make sure the line has been fitted and that the coupling nut that attaches to the ballcock tailpiece slides onto the tube (threads up) first. Follow that by a compression nut (threads down), and then the compression ring, before you attach it to the shutoff valve. Take care not to mar the compression nut with a wrench. After connecting the supply line to the ballcock inlet, turn on the water line and check for leaks.

Toilet flange

If you're lucky, your project didn't disturb the toilet flange. If you have to install a new one, the following information will prove helpful. Start by removing the floor covering around the soil hole and trial fit the toilet flange in the hole. If you have to enlarge the hole to accept the flange, use an electric reciprocating saw. Cut only enough of the rough opening for the flange to slide over the soil pipe and rest on the finish floor. If you cut out too much, the screws that hold the flange to the floor will have nothing to bite into.

If your soil pipe is higher than the finish floor, cut it off an ample ¾ in. below the finish floor using an inside pipe cutter or an abrasive cutting disk. Place the cutting disk on the inside of the pipe and make the cut from inside to outside.

When you are comfortable with the trial fit, permanently attach the flange to the soil pipe. Make sure the holes for the toilet bolts are parallel to the wall so the toilet tank will sit square to the wall. Whatever type of solvent cement you use, make sure it's the right solvent cement for your soil pipe—ABS or PVC. Twist the flange slightly and press it to the floor over the soil pipe all in one motion; once it is in place, don't play with it. Then screw the flange to the floor and put plumber's putty around the bolts in order to secure them.

When beveling the hole to match the bevel around the bottom side of the flange, use a reciprocating saw; be aware of the saw's shoe as you don't want it to damage the floor covering.

New Toilet Bowl Rings

In my bathroom I used a new toilet bowl ring that eliminates the wax ring. Wax-Free Bowl Gasket™ by Fluidmaster® is designed to fit both 3-in. and 4-in. drainpipes. It also eliminates the need for stacking multiple wax rings on new or raised flooring. The cardboard spacer, designed to collapse and stay in place, allows the bowl horn to contact the gasket opening before the bowl touches the finish floor. It's an easy-to-install complete system, but on a tile floor it will not secure the toilet enough to prevent movement. If you decide to use this wax-free gasket and have a tile floor, caulk under the base all the way around.

This O-ring seals tightly to block sewer gases.

The rubber gasket and O-ring prevent splash-up.

PRO TIP

PRO TIP

As you caulk around the toilet, leave a small opening in the back so the water will have an escape route if the toilet should leak through the wax ring.

IN DETAIL

When setting a toilet on a tile floor, it's important to turn the bowl upside down and check to see that the base is flat and contains no high spots. If any feet are higher than the outside base perimeter, the base will not sit squarely on the floor. As a result the toilet will rock on the floor after it is fully installed. To eliminate this, grind down the tops of the feet to the level point of the outside base perimeter with a small abrasive disk in an electric drill. This isn't as easy as it sounds—work carefully and patiently.

When attaching screws through all the holes in the flange, be sure to use coarse-threaded screws.

After tightening the toilet bolts, carefully cut them off with a minihacksaw.

Setting the toilet

Begin by installing the wax bowl ring. Take the time to make sure the ring is seated properly. If necessary, use your hands to work and press the room temperature wax to the flange. I find it easier to fit the ring to the toilet flange and then to lower the toilet on top of it.

When you are ready to set the toilet, turn the bowl on its side to familiarize yourself with the location of the opening (horn) that will fit into the wax ring. Then straddle the bowl with your knees, pick up the toilet, and place it over the bolts and into the wax ring. Once in place, twist the toilet slightly and press down so it sits perpendicular to the wall. Double check this placement by making sure the distance between each bolt

and the wall is the same. Apply pressure to the toilet until it compresses the wax ring and is firmly seated on the floor.

The next step in the installation is to secure the toilet to the flange, but the hardware must be in the correct order—bolt cap bases, washers, nuts—so you can properly tighten the nuts. Secure the nuts little by little—don't completely tighten one and then the other. Take care not to overtighten—it's a sure way to crack the base. Carefully cut the excess bolts off with a minihacksaw, vacuum up the metal filings, and mount the bolt caps.

To install the tank, mount the spud washer over the flush valve tailpiece on the tank's underside. Lift the tank onto the back of the bowl, centering the spud washer over the water inlet opening.

Line up the bolt holes and either slide the rubber washers (your toilet may differ) over the bolts before inserting them into the holes or insert the bolts into the rubber sleeves. Use a slotted screwdriver in the tank to secure the bolts while you tighten the nuts on the underside evenly with a nut driver. Don't tighten one nut and then move to the next, or overtighten—you can crack the tank. If the lid doesn't sit squarely, attach self-adhesive foam strips to the lid's underside.

Carefully tighten the nuts to the toilet seat, especially if you use pliers for leverage. The bowl will crack if the nuts are overtightened. Finger tight is normally not good enough, so take your time and use groove-joint pliers with plastic inserts in the jaws so the nuts aren't marred.

Your bathroom is now almost finished, but there are still a few more items to be completed. In Chapter Ten I talk about the final touches and go into detail about caulking.

Dressing the Toilet

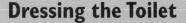

After viewing what seemed like zillions of toilets, we chose Memoirs, a two-piece round-bowl square-base toilet by Kohler that conjured up a 1930s feel. It was just what we needed to tie the theme of the entire bathroom together. Believe it or not, our bathroom design started with the stock wooden toilet seat pictured below that we bought at our local home center. It was finished in the medium cherry stain we wanted, and the light-colored central inlay was just a bonus. Its chrome hinge system even matches the chrome of the new Price Pfister® flush lever assembly. The wood design handle was refinished both to match the toilet seat and to complete the look. You never know what will spark a project's design—it can even be a toilet seat.

Tall and narrow, Memoirs® by Kohler® has a nostalgic feel. Its state-of-the-art Ingenium™ (Siphon Jet) flushing system uses just 1.6 gallons per flush.

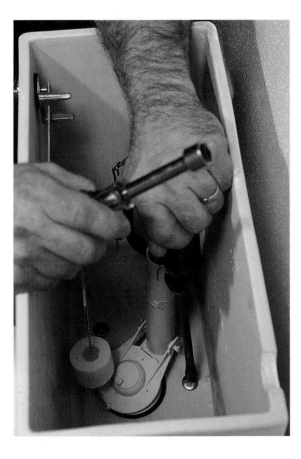

I discovered a small leak, so I drained the tank. In the photo at left, I'm using a slotted screwdriver and a nut driver to tighten the bolt where the leak appeared around the nut on the underside of the bowl.

Finishing

CHAPTER TEN

Touches

1 Final Prep Work, p. 154

The final stage of remodeling has arrived. In this chapter, I'll share professional tips on prep work and caulking as well as installing door and cabinet hardware and bathroom accessories. The section on caulking is very important—I encourage you to read it carefully before you pick up the caulking gun because proper caulk application will have a big impact on your bathroom's final appearance. Now is not the time to skimp on the quality of the products you choose or the care you take in using them. It's essential that you apply caulk properly and allow it sufficient drying time to cure. Otherwise, you may have water failure around tile, the tub/shower enclosure, and the shower door track. This phase of the project should not be hurried.

Finishing touches can make or break the final appearance of your bathroom, so take special care in detailing; it's an essential part of high-quality workmanship.

2 Caulking, p. 155

3 Installing Door Hardware, p. 159

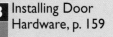

4 Installing Cabinet Hardware, p. 162

5 Mounting Accessories, p. 164

PRO TIP

Experiment with wood fillers on wood of the same type as your countertop edge until you find one that accepts the stain and dries to match.

TRADE SECRET

There are times when it's not wise to use wood filler before applying stain and finish. Your eye is drawn to conspicuous nail holes that result when the filler doesn't take the stain. Instead, use a non-hardening putty stick or pencil in a color to match the stain. After working the putty into the holes, remove any excess with mineral spirits on a white towel and smooth the putty flush with the surface. In some cases you may need a second application to fill the hole flush with the surface. It takes some practice to get it just right.

When working with stain, use blue painter's masking tape to protect the wall and cover the finish floor.

Final Prep Work

In this section I'll explain how to finish the countertop edges, the door casings, and the crown molding. This is where you'll learn the professional tricks that will make your bathroom a masterpiece.

Finishing countertop edges

When fabricating a laminate countertop with wooden edges, the proper filler, stain, and finish will make a difference in the appearance of the completed edge and in its durability.

Set the nails deep enough so that the holes will hold a sandable amount of stainable wood filler. Use a 1-in. putty knife to apply it. If the filler shrinks, apply more. Sand the filler using a hand-held rubber sanding block, beginning with 100-grit sandpaper. Check for scratches afterward, and use finer grit sandpaper to sand them out. Use a 1-in. disposable brush to apply stain near the wall, and put on the rest using a white cotton rag. If the filler dries to a different color than the stained edge, use a furniture touch-up marker to fix it. Experiment on a sample piece to obtain a perfect match. After the filler dries, apply two

Once you are satisfied with the joint you have sanded, feather out the paint with your sanding block.

coats of clear finish. I prefer lacquer because it can be applied with a brush, it dries fast, and it can be sanded with 220-grit white sandpaper in about five minutes—and then you'll be ready for that second coat. Next, resand and rub out the surface using #0000 (very fine) steel wool.

Door casings and crown molding

Finish work can be tedious, but it's a necessary phase of any home remodeling project. Door casings and crown molding are so visible that extra care needs to be taken to get perfect results.

Door casings. There is no guarantee that a joint will come together at a miter as anticipated. There are several possible reasons: perhaps the molding pieces are not uniformly thick; the door-jamb may be off a bit so the casing doesn't sit evenly at the joint; or the wall's surface may not be flat and true in the area where the casing pieces meet. In my bathroom the jamb was off, so I sanded the miter cuts at the joint, using a sanding block to achieve a matching joint.

Crown molding. The same situation may occur with crown molding. It's a good idea when installing crown molding, especially when wallpaper is involved, to paint it beforehand. Just remember that all fillers and latex caulk require priming before applying the final touch-up coat of paint. Investing time in all moldings—casing or crown—yields natural looking joints.

Caulking

Caulk serves two purposes: it seals areas from moisture and it provides an aesthetically pleasing finish around fixtures and countertops. The caulk you choose and how well you apply it could make or break the final appearance of your bathroom.

Caulks come in three basic formulas—latex, siliconized acrylic latex, and 100 percent silicone—and a range of colors. I recommend that you use a caulking gun with a silicone (rubber)

caulk cartridge. Latex caulks should be applied by hand from a soft-squeeze tube. Apply caulk in the tub and shower enclosures, around a shower door, toilet, and sink, and on backsplashes. If you've installed a handrail, caulk around the hardware where it attaches to the enclosure or the wall. It's important that 100 percent silicone not be used on any surface that may later require paint because it does not accept paint well.

Cut the nozzle on the tube of caulk at a comfortable angle and as small as you can. Apply the caulk in one direction; don't squeeze out too much, work quickly, and don't play with it—especially silicone. Latex or siliconized acrylic latex are easy to work with: just apply a bead of caulk, wipe the excess with your finger, then wipe the area clean with a barely-wet sponge and follow it with your finger again. Wipe your finger on a white rag or paper towel after each pass.

When you are satisfied with the results—and this is going to be hard—I recommend you not use any facilities (such as the shower) where caulk has been applied until the caulk has fully cured. Curing times for different caulks are given on the canister, along with other useful information.

Sealing enclosures

Enclosure walls—whether in the tub/shower area or shower stall—all need to be sealed with caulk in the corners and wherever they meet at the tub and shower pan.

Finishing the shower door

A leak-free shower door can add years to the life of your new bathroom. Caulk plays a very important role in making sure the door's components don't leak; if the shower door's track, or "curb," is improperly caulked, it becomes the prime suspect in cases where leaks occur.

It's important to work slowly and allow sufficient drying time between installing each shower

PRO TIP

When you cut the nozzle on the tube of caulk, initially trim it as small as you can— the smaller the bead of caulk, the easier it is to work with.

IN DETAIL

Should you caulk the tub/shower enclosure where it meets the wall? Yes—it helps to seal against moisture and it unifies the kit with the wall visually, even if the wall is painted or wallpapered. Use latex or siliconized acrylic latex. The trick when working on painted walls is to wipe excess caulk off the wall with a clean sponge. Dry the area with a white towel and check to make sure no caulk haze remains. (Repainting is the only way to eliminate the haze.) For wallpapered walls apply blue painter's masking tape the length of the surface close to the line you'll be caulking, and then carefully remove the tape after you've caulked. Professionally speaking, I prefer to use a siliconized acrylic latex caulk where water will be visible and a latex caulk where paint will be involved.

It's easier to caulk before the tub spout is installed. Here I'm applying a polybond (siliconized acrylic latex) by Lighthouse® Products.

Use either your index finger or pinkie to wipe off excess caulk. Make sure your finger is clean and your nail is short.

door component. Use rubber silicone to assemble the components, especially the track and other areas where there could be standing water. Silicone works well to seal inside the track where it meets the frame at the wall (wall jambs). Leaks can occur at both ends of the tub/shower, but they're more likely where the track meets the plumbing wall.

To ensure that your shower door will be a leak-proof system, you'll want to follow the instruc-

tions in the manual that accompanied it. Here are some general guidelines.

Vertical doorjambs. Siliconized acrylic latex can be used for both the interior and exterior sides of the vertical shower doorjambs. Use silicone to seal the area on the interior side where it sits on the curb of the tub and where the track will sit. (This area is crucial because water often puddles there, especially on the showerhead side.) Clean the area first using rubbing alcohol and

Caulk the interior and exterior sides of both shower door-jambs using a siliconized acrylic latex, including the face (interior and exterior) of the header and up and over it where it meets the enclosure at both ends.

then apply a silicone caulk. After it sits overnight, apply a second coat, if needed. Repeat with the exterior sides of the jambs. If you use white silicone, as I did, take time to smooth the silicone because this is a visible area. It, too, may require a second application.

Cleanouts. Because the Senza (Kohler) cleanouts (on track ends) were black, I applied clear silicone to the inside of the wall jambs where the cleanouts butt up to them and

to the tub surfaces on which the cleanouts will rest.

Apply silicone caulk to the track's underside and install the track. Clean up any caulk that has oozed out, and smooth the caulk surface with your finger. Do not fill any gaps at this time. After about four hours, clean the area with rubbing alcohol. Allow the track to sit overnight, and recaulk it where it meets the tub's surface. Because these areas are visible, carefully smooth the caulk.

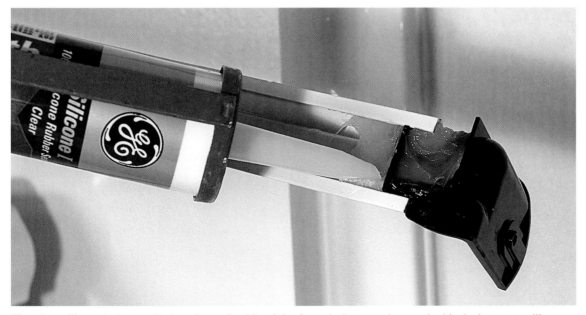

The clear silicone being applied to the underside of the Senza's door track over the black cleanouts will cure for seven days before the track is installed.

Less is more when applying caulk—you can always add a second layer the following day.

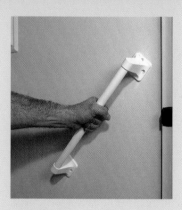

IN DETAIL

Grab bars are a must for tub/shower areas. Locate one on the wall opposite the plumbing wall in a position that is comfortable as you enter and exit. In our bathroom, I angled it to match the way we reach for it when exiting the tub. Install the grab bar according to the manufacturer's recommendations. (You'll need to use a masonry drill bit for tile.) In wet areas, caulk under the screw heads that hold the bar in place. Apply matching siliconized acrylic latex caulk around the trim pieces that sit up against the enclosure wall. If your grab bar fits into the support elbow that's not part of a one-piece unit, the bar requires caulk where it meets the elbow to prevent water from entering the elbow.

After waiting a day for my white silicone to set up, I caulked around the cleanouts with clear silicone.

Sealing the backsplash

Where the backsplash meets the countertop requires sealing so water doesn't siphon behind it and ruin the cabinet, countertop, and wall. It is also a highly visible area, so take care to select a siliconized acrylic latex in an appropriate color to match your grout.

Caulk one side of the wall first—adjacent walls are caulked the following day, after the first day's caulk application has set up. Use a finger to smooth the caulk, removing as much as possible. Remove any excess caulk using a sponge dipped in warm water and wrung out. Make sure to rinse the sponge in clean water and wring it out after each wipe to prevent leaving a stubborn caulk haze.

The caulk line should match the width of the grout lines. If caulk gets onto your grout lines, use a cotton swab soaked in warm water to clean it

off. Then dip your finger in warm water and run the tip of it over the caulk line one more time for a smooth, uniform finish.

Sealing washbasins. Surface-mounted or undermounted sinks need to be sealed, too. Once a surface-mounted washbasin has been installed, run a bead of siliconized acrylic latex caulk around the perimeter where it meets the countertop. The caulk prevents water from seeping under the washbasin and provides an aesthetically pleasing finish.

Once a bead of latex or siliconized acrylic latex caulk has been applied around the perimeter of the washbasin where it meets the countertop, trace over it with your index finger. Follow the perimeter and wipe your finger on a white towel along the way. Use a wet sponge to clean up the excess and smooth the caulk line at the same time. You may have to make more than one pass with the sponge, rinsing it in clean water after each pass, to remove the haze. If necessary, make a final pass with a moist fingertip for a smooth finish.

The caulk is a little heavy, but since it's a siliconized acrylic latex caulk you can use a sponge to correctly shape the caulk line.

Sealing Tubs and Toilets

Color Caulk manufactures a siliconized acrylic latex in colors to match all ceramic tile grouts. It's available sanded or unsanded. Grout would be a poor choice to use up against the tub; caulk is a better solution.

It's important to seal the front of the tub or shower pan where it meets the floor. I find silicone caulk works well if vinyl floor covering is involved, but siliconized acrylic latex is better suited for tile floors. Silicones are limited in colors, but latex caulks are available in a rainbow of colors that will blend into the floor better than white caulk. White sometimes stands out so much that it becomes intrusive, an effect you do not want to create.

Another area of concern is around the base of the toilet. I caulk the base, as required by the code, and especially in the following situations: if the toilet sits on a tile floor; if a special bowl ring (not a wax ring) is used; if there is some lateral movement with the toilet; or if aesthetics are an issue.

Installing Door Hardware

When you purchase a door, check the edge (stile) of the bore side to see how the door was prepped for the backset. Some manufacturers will bore a hole for a "drive-in" latch bolt (backset), or they will mortise an area for a latch plate. Backsets come in either style, and some contain an optional plate that can convert a drive-in latch to a latch plate, so it's a good idea to check the lockset before purchasing it. In my bathroom I installed a prehung door, described in Chapter Eight, that was prebored for a handle and backset, and its jamb was mortised for a strike plate.

The backset

The backset I installed has a permanent security plate with a finished-trim latch plate, all fastened together with two matching screws. My door

Here the fabricator applies siliconized acrylic latex caulk to a Swanstone® washbasin undermounted in a granite top. This caulk is required by undermount washbasins to prevent water from splashing into the cabinet.

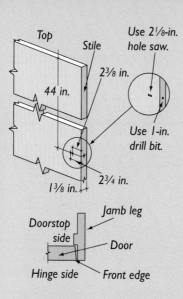

Top
Stile
Use 2⅛-in. hole saw.
2⅜ in.
44 in.
Use 1-in. drill bit.
2¾ in.
1⅜ in.

Jamb leg
Doorstop side
Door
Hinge side — Front edge

IN DETAIL

To bore for a handle in a newly installed door blank, close the door and lightly mark its face with a pencil even with the existing strike plate's center, usually 44 in. down from the top. Use an adjustable square to transfer the mark to the stile's center and to the door face at 2⅜ or 2¾ in. (backset length) from the stile's tapered front edge (hinge side). Use a 1-in. Forstner-style wood bit to drill in the center of the stile for the backset. For the handle, drill a 2⅛-in. hole using a hole saw through one side until the bit pierces the other side. Then drill from this side where the bit hole appears to prevent damage to the door skin.

The drive-in latch hole needs to be mortised for our latch with its security plate and finished trim.

When installing the handle assemblies, first do the knob that has the screw stems, and then do its mate. Make sure the lock (it has screw holes in the trim) is on the correct side of the door.

Drill a pilot hole to prevent the stile from splitting, and put in the screws by hand—don't use a power screwdriver.

required mortising to accept this unit. To mark an area to be mortised, I would normally turn the backset around and insert it backward into the 1-in. prebored hole to bring the latch plate flat against the stile so I could trace around it. My finished-trim latch plate was removable, however, so I was able to center the plate on the 1-in. hole and within the edges of the stile, and then trace around it using a pencil (not an ink pen).

To mortise, use a ½-in. or ¾-in. wide chisel and carefully chisel out a 1-in. by 2¼-in. area (for a 1⅜-in.-wide door) that's deep enough to accept the security plate and/or finished-trim latch plate. Make sure the chisel is sharp; there's no room for error. After a trial fit, install the backset so the curve on the latch bolt faces the direction the door closes. To center pilot holes in the latch plate, use a self-centering drill bit with a bit diameter one or two sizes under final screw size.

Handle assemblies

To install the handle assemblies, start with the knob that has the screw stems (doorstop side of the door), and then its mate. Make sure the lock, which has screw holes in the trim, is on the correct side of the door, normally the inside. Install the two screws and tighten them just enough so that you can still move the handle. Grab both knobs and gently slide the entire unit up and down a few times until you determine the center point of the 2⅛-in. hole. When you are satisfied, tighten—but don't overtighten—the screws. Use a screwdriver with a long skinny shank so as not to damage the finish on the knobs. Before testing the door, mark, mortise, and drill for the strike plate on the corresponding jamb. If you have a strike plate with square corners, use a chisel to square the round corners of the premortised area so the strike plate will fit.

Always predrill holes for the strike using a self-centered drill bit to prevent the jamb from splitting. If the door does not latch, reinstall the strike closer to the door. If the door is loose after it is closed, reinstall the strike closer to the doorstops or bend the tongue on the strike toward the doorstop using pliers with nylon jaws. Remember to remove all hardware before painting.

Doorstops

There are all kinds of doorstops available on the market, but I find a base-mount doorstop, i.e., one that fastens to the base molding, to be most effective. However, you'll need to have planned ahead for it by installing a backer board for the doorstop during the framing stage, especially if the base molding is rubber or vinyl.

Because I installed a tile base, a plastic plug anchor was required. I used a masonry bit to drill a hole in the face of the tile. The next step was to tap in the plastic anchor with a hammer. Work carefully, though, because hitting the face of the

Doorstop Options

This solid base-mount doorstop is also available in a spring version. Remove the rubber bumper and tighten the doorstop with a wrench. Do not overtighten or the tile could crack. Here the doorstop is fastened closer to the edge of the tile—its hardest part.

Don't overlook the importance of doorstops in protecting your new walls. Several types are available. The first, a wall doorstop, requires a backer board at the height of the handle and between two studs. The backer board provides support for the doorstop and prevents the door handle from punching the doorstop through the wall. The second is the floor-mount doorstop, a good choice when there is no wall behind the open door. There's also the hinge-pin doorstop, my least favorite. This type of doorstop has a tendency over time to loosen the hinge pin or to prevent the pin from sitting in its required position. Also, the bumpers on both ends of the doorstop can damage the door casing as well as the face of the door. This type of doorstop works well temporarily until a permanent doorstop can be installed.

If you've planned to use a floor-mount doorstop on a floor with radiant heat, it's important to mark wire locations before installing the finish floor.

IN DETAIL

Tip-out trays come in stainless steel or plastic and in basic white or an almond color. The almond plastic tray pictured below is an extruded tip-out tray cut to fit the maximum length of the front of the cabinet, but which still clears the cabinet frame behind it on both ends. Because of its length, I installed this tray without its hardware, so I plan to add a small chain on the left-hand side to prevent the front from tipping out too far.

IN DETAIL

If you have to fill screw holes to make an adjustment, plug the holes using glue and one or more toothpicks. Re-drill the hole once the glue has dried.

Before installing the doorstop, check the backside of the flange area where the screw is mounted to see if there is a recessed area to accept the plastic anchor's head. If not, use a chisel and cut off the head so the anchor is flush with the tile's surface.

tile could cause it to crack. To install my doorstop, I removed the rubber bumper and tightened the doorstop with a wrench. It's easy in this situation to tighten too much, but don't—the tile could crack.

Installing Cabinet Hardware

Whether you purchased prebuilt cabinets or had them custom made, as we did, you still may have to attach hardware. Our cabinetmaker intentionally left off the doors so they wouldn't be damaged as I worked. Take precautions with your own cabinetry so that you don't mar its surface.

Doors

It's easier to hang cabinet doors, both upper and lower, with the cabinet on its back, but it can still be done after installation. The trick is to have a helper and to install only the top screws of each hinge. That way, if you have to adjust the door by moving the hinge, you have only one hole per hinge to plug and re-drill.

Handles

To attach the handles, first drill the door or drawer front to accept the handle screws. It's best to drill from the front, but be sure to place a block of wood on the back where the drill bit will come through. Without the block, the drill bit will blow out the back, causing damage to the finish. Turn the screws by hand and do not tighten too far—in softer wood this will cause the base of the handle to dig into the wood. Also, the screw could break off inside the handle, possibly making it useless. Finally, don't forget to install bumpers on the upper and lower inside corners of the doors (on the same side as the handles).

For drawer fronts, center the bumpers on the inside of the two vertical ends where the fronts hit the cabinet stiles.

A recessed toilet paper holder

I chose to install a recessed toilet paper holder on the side of the cabinet to provide a little more space between it and the seat. Installing one takes some time and special care; you don't want to damage the face of the cabinet with the jigsaw that's required to

Drill pilot holes with a self-centered drill bit and install the screws on your cabinet hinges by hand.

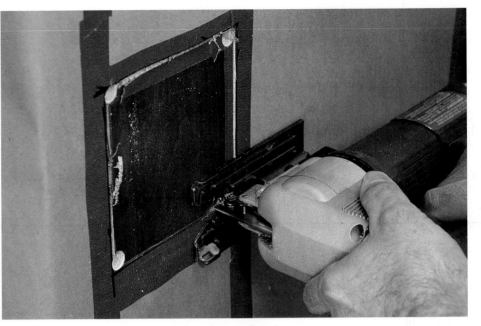

Don't apply a lot of pressure against the jigsaw while it cuts.

cut the hole. Once you determine the rough opening, attach brown paper with painter's blue masking tape, using enough tape to cover where you plan to cut. Next, mark the right location with a permanent marker on the masking tape. Using a ½-in. Forstner-style wood bit, drill holes in the cabinet face in each corner so the point of the bit just penetrates the inside of the cabinet. Working from the inside of the cabinet, place the bit in the pilot hole and complete the drilling.

Moving to the outside of the cabinet, score around the markings with a utility knife. Set the orbital jigsaw in 0 mode (to prevent the orbital action). Place the blade in one of the holes and start cutting just inside the score line to prevent the surface from chipping. Once you've cut, clean the cutout by lightly sanding the inside and outside edges, and then place the backer plate on the inside of the cabinet so it straddles the cutout—with the feet in a vertical position. Have a helper hold it in place while you work from the front to

The backer plate may have to be repositioned so the holes line up when you place screws from the front through the paper holder.

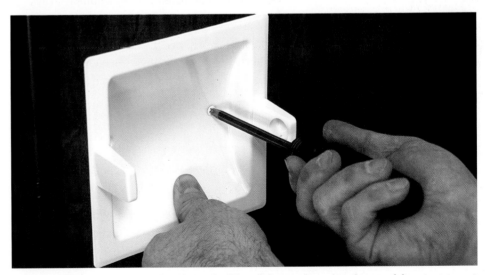

Because these screws are painted, gently tighten them using a hand screwdriver to prevent damage to the screwhead.

IN DETAIL

No matter how detailed your preplanning, you'll probably decide within a month after finishing your bathroom to hang a new accessory or one that never got hung. At this point you might not remember where all the studs and backer boards are located. This won't be a problem if you have a studfinder, like the Triscanner® by Zircon®. This unit scans deep for metal and can find studs and joists with both a light locator and sound. I used it to find and check backer board width to determine where to install a hook because the measurement had not been written down in our original plans.

Detailing a Recessed Paper Holder

The screws of a recessed toilet paper holder may be so long that they penetrate the backer plate inside the vanity cabinet. If these screws extend out far enough, you could injure yourself if you reach into the cabinet. Take time to prep this area to make it user-friendly. Use a mini-hacksaw to cut the screws to a length that will accept a vinyl or rubber cap—an easy way to ensure safety.

This is an accident waiting to happen.

install the holder. Hold it still, otherwise it will scratch the cabinet. Place the screws through the paper holder and into the backer plate.

Mounting Accessories

This has to be the best part of the entire project: mounting mirrors, pictures, and towel bars and rings. Take care as you install these items to properly secure them so they don't fall off the wall. Funny as it sounds, this occurs quite often.

Towel bars and rings

When installing towel bars and other similar fixtures such as a towel ring, soap dish, and tissue holder, it is a good idea to use a level. When you are satisfied with the fixture's placement, use an awl to mark the wall. Push the awl through the screw holes and on into the wallboard.

After marking the accessory's placement on the wall, determine if there is a stud or other solid backing by drilling a hole (using a drill bit smaller than the screws you plan to install). If you've determined that there is no solid material behind the hole, redrill it to accept an anchor, such as one by Toggler. With the anchor in place, insert the red key (plunger) into the hole and push to pop the anchor open behind the hollow wall.

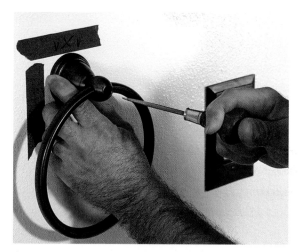

An awl—a handy tool—marks the wall where the screw for the towel ring will be fastened.

If you hit solid material, predrill the hole with a drill bit at a size smaller than your screws to prevent one from snapping off during final installation.

Mirrors and pictures

Mirrors are similar to pictures——they help to balance the wall aesthetically. For up-close viewing, a side- or a wall-mounted pullout mirror might be desirable in your bathroom. Just remember that all wall-mounted mirrors and pictures have to be hung using specialized hardware to prevent them from falling.

Hanging mirrors. Large wall mirrors can be difficult to hang, so be sure to buy top-quality hardware. One option is to use two heavy-duty mirror hangers that attach to the back of the frame with two screws. If your backer board was miscalculated, or if you never got around to installing it, use a metal single-point self-drilling wallboard anchor by ITW Buildex that screws in without requiring a pilot hole. Then, with the screws protruding from the anchors a bit, use the hangers on the back of the mirror to loop up and over the screws.

Hanging pictures. Pictures have their own set of rules. The size of the picture determines whether you'll need a single picture wire or two picture hangers. Nails cannot provide secure support for large pictures. Consider instead the EverStraight® picture-hanging system that uses a screw to secure the hanger. It's designed to be used with hanging wire, which is what I used for the picture in my bathroom, but it's also suitable for a sawtooth hanger or a metal frame, so I can change the picture in the future and not worry about the type of hardware that's supporting it.

Turning the lights on

Now that the job is complete, check to make sure that everything in your new bathroom works correctly: heat, light, and water. Check all water connections, fixtures, and tub/shower doors for leaks, and look for places where touch-ups might be required, especially around areas where tile and grout were applied. You might have to bring out your paintbrush again, although sometimes just a cotton swab will work.

Now is also the time to call for a final inspection from your local building department.

I hope your remodeling project turned out as well as the dream bathroom you pictured. Take a moment to pat yourself on the back for a job well done—and enjoy that new bathroom!

I feel more comfortable when I position a picture knowing I've used quality hardware.

Here's the finished project. Our bathroom is only 5 ft. by 9 ft., but it looks twice the size.

Resources

Chapter One:
Repair or Remodel?

Easter Seals
230 West Monroe St., Suite 1800
Chicago, IL 60606
312-726-6200
800-221-6827 (toll-free)
(TTY): 312-726-4258
www.easter-seals.org

Architectural and Transportation
    Barriers Compliance Board
1331 F St. N.W., Suite 1000
Washington, DC 20004-1111
(Voice/TDD): 800-872-2253
(TTY): 800-993-2822
www.access-board.gov

Center for Accessible Housing
    School of Design
North Carolina State University,
    Box 8613
Raleigh, NC 27695
(Voice/TDD): 919-737-3082
www.design.ncsu.edu/cud

Paralyzed Veterans of America
801 18th St., N.W.
Washington, DC 20006-3516
800-424-8200
www.pva.org

United Spinal Association
75-20 Astoria Boulevard
Jackson Heights, NY 11370
718-803-3782
www.unitedspinal.org

Dept. of Justice—ADA
800-514-0301
(TTY): 800-514-0383
www.usdoj.gov/crt/ada/
    adahom1.htm

Bosch Power Tools
4300 West Peterson Ave.
Chicago, IL 60646
877-267-2499
www.boschtools.com

The Swan Corporation
One City Centre, Suite 2300
St. Louis, MO 63101
800-325-7008
www.swanstome.com

Hy-Lite Products, Inc.
101 California Avenue
Beaumont, CA 92223
800-827-3691
www.hy-lite.com

RIDGID Tool Company
400 Clark St.
Elyria, OH 44036
888-743-4333
www.ridgid.com

DeWalt
701 E. Joppa Rd., TW425
Baltimore, MD 21286
800-433-9258
www.dewalt.com

APA—The Engineered Wood
    Association
7011 S. 19th
Tacoma, WA 98466
253-565-6600
www.apawood.org

Chapter Two:
Demolition and Framing

Occupational Safety &
    Health Administration
200 Constitution Avenue, NW
Washington, DC 20210
800-321-6742
www.osha.gov

US Environmental
    Protection Agency
Ariel Rios Building
1200 Pennsylvania Ave., NW
Washington, DC 20460
202-272-0167
www.epa.gov

Milwaukee Electric Tool
    Corporation
13135 West Lisbon Rd.
Brookfield, WI 53005
800-729-3878
www.milwaukeetools.com

Hy-Lite Products, Inc.
101 California Avenue
Beaumont, CA 92223
800-827-3691
www.hy-lite.com

Quik Drive USA, Inc.
436 Calvert Drive
Gallatin, TN 37066
888-487-7845
www.quikdrive.com

Jacuzzi Inc.
2121 N. California Blvd.,
    Ste. 475
Walnut Creek, CA 94596
800-288-4002
www.jacuzzi.com

Chapter Three:
Plumbing Rough-in

NIBCO Inc.
1516 Middlebury St.
Elkhart, IN 46516-4740
574-295-3000
www.nibco.com

Price Pfister, Inc.
19701 DaVinci
Foothill Ranch, CA 92610
800-732-8238 (Consumer
    Service Department)
www.pricepfister.com

Fernco, Inc.
300 South Dayton St.
Davison, MI 48423
800-521-1283
www.fernco.com

Chapter Four:
Electrical Rough-in

Sun Touch
2867 W. Chestnut Expressway
Springfield, MO 65802
888-432-8932
www.suntouch.net

Custom Building Products
    Corporate
13001 Seal Beach Blvd.
Seal Beach, CA 90740-2753
800-272-8786
www.custombuildingproducts.com

Deflect-o Corp
7035 E. 86th St.
P.O. Box 50057
Indianapolis, IN 46250
800-428-4328
www.deflecto.com

Chapter Five:
Working with Wallboard

Johns Manville
P.O. Box 5108
Denver, CO 80217-5108
800-654-3103
www.jm.com

The Stanley Works
Goldblatt
480 Myrtle St.
New Britain, CT 06050
860-225-5111
www.stanleyworks.com

Zinsser Co., Inc.
173 Belmont Dr.
Somerset, NJ 08875
732-469-8100
www.zinsser.com

Chapter Six:
Flooring, Cabinets,
and Countertops

Marshalltown Trowel Company
104 South 8th Ave.
Marshalltown, IA 50158
800-987-6935/641-753-5999
www.marshalltown.com

Mario & Son, Inc.
6523 E. Main Avenue
Spokane, WA 99212
877-536-6079
www.marioandson.com

Chapter Seven:
Tub and Shower
Enclosures

The Swan Corporation
One City Centre, Suite 2300
St. Louis, MO 63101
800-325-7008
www.swanstome.com

Tile Council of America, Inc.
100 Clemson Research Blvd.
Anderson, SC 29625
864-646-8453
www.tileusa.com

Porter-Cable Corporation
4825 Highway 45 North
P.O. Box 2468
Jackson, TN 38302-2468
800-487-8665
www.porter-cable.com

Kohler Co.
444 Highland Drive
Kohler, WI 53044
800-456-4537
www.kohler.com

Chapter Eight:
Doors and Moldings

Fypon
960 West Barre Rd.
Archbold, Ohio 43502
800-446-3040
www.fypon.com

Chapter Nine:
Finishing Up
with Fixtures

Waterpik Technologies
1730 East Prospect Rd.
Fort Collins, CO 80553
800-766-4283
www.waterpik.com

Fluidmaster Inc.
30800 Rancho Viejo Rd.
San Juan Capistrano, CA 92675
(800) 631-2011
www.fluidmaster.com

Chapter Ten:
Finishing Touches

GE Sealants & Adhesives
16325 Northcross Drive
Huntersville, NC 28078
800-626-2000
www.gesealants.com

DAP Inc.
2400 Boston St., Suite 200
Baltimore, MD 21224
800-543-3840
www.dap.com

Color Caulk, Inc.
3148 Roanoke Rd.
Kansas City, MO 64111
800-875-8453
www.colorcaulk.com

Toggler Anchor System
Div. of Mechanical Plastics Corp.
444 Saw Mill River Rd.
P.O. Box 554
Elmsford, NY 10523
888-864-4537
www.toggler.com

ITW Buildex
1349 West Bryn Mawr Avenue
Itasca, IL 60143
800-284-5339
www.itwbuildex.com

Zircon Corporation
1580 Dell Avenue
Campbell, CA 95008
800-245-9265
www.zircon.com

Visit the author's website for the
items listed below:

C.R.S., Inc.
P.O. Box 4567
Spokane, WA 99220
509-926-1724
www.asktooltalk.com

Contractor's Helping Hands
Packet (Chapter 1);
Rockeater (Chapter 5);
Grout Grabber (Chapter 7);
EverStraight Picture Hangers,
(Chapter 10).

Index